Indian Polity and Economy

A Mirror to Difficult Times

Also from frontpage

PRANAB BARDHAN

Globalisation, Democracy and Corruption
An Indian Perspective

Indian Polity and Economy
A Mirror to Difficult Times

Pranab Bardhan

frontpage

frontpage

https://frontpagepublications.com

First published 2021

Frontpage Publications Limited
Level 2, 13 John Prince's Street, London W1G 0JR, United Kingdom

Frontpage
Level B, 76 B B Ganguly Street, Kolkata 700012, India

© Pranab Bardhan

British Library Cataloguing in Publishing Data
A catalogue record for this book is available from the British Library

ISBN: 978 93 81043 46 2

Printed in India
By Sadhana Udyog
26D Balaram Ghosh Street, Kolkata 700004, India

Typeset by Sonal Mansata
85 Park Street, Kolkata 700016, India

Contents

Preface

Over the last several years Indian polity and economy are going through tumultuous times, even before the pandemic hit us. There has been, of course, the legacy of long-standing structural problems. On top of this, we are now being ruled by a political leadership that is not merely the most divisive and undemocratic in Independent India's history, but also highly incompetent in vital matters, partly because it rewards loyalty over competence in its officials, is highly over-centralised, and more prone to hype than serious implementation. Then when the pandemic came, it went for the theatrics of the world's severest lockdown without consideration about what would happen to the masses of poor people who were rendered suddenly unemployed and abandoned, and then generally mismanaging the health crisis over several months, so that in some sense India today is one of world's worst victims of the pandemic.

Much of this period I have been disturbed by these trends in the Indian polity and economy, and the short essays in this book reflect my despair and anguish. But I hope they also reflect my considered views on what is going wrong, and an analysis of the underlying political economy, which may suggest some ways out for the younger readers of this book. Since most of the essays came out as topical op-eds in various outlets in response to the evolving situation, there is an immediacy to the treatment which varies with the context. There is some repetition, which I have decided to keep in order not to interrupt the flow of arguments in each case.

There is also a whole section on a major directional change in India's welfare policy—towards universal basic income—that I have advocated for more than a decade. In this sense I hope this book serves not just as a mirror to the current events that are not very pretty, but also a signpost toward changes for the better. To paraphrase something Rabindranath Tagore said in his impassioned last testament in 1941, *The Crisis of Civilisation*, we must not take this seemingly endless defeat of the spirit of humanity as our final destiny.

Grateful acknowledgment is due to the various publishers of the original pieces and to Abhijit Mazumder for his invaluable efforts in collecting them and pressing me to bring them out in a coherent form in this book.

Berkeley, September 2020   Pranab Bardhan

POLITICAL-ECONOMY AND POLICY

Challenges for a
Minimum Social Democracy in India

Economic & Political Weekly, 5 March 2011

More than six decades after the establishment of the Indian Republic (which is constitutionally declared as 'socialist'), even the barest minimum social protection remains unavailable for its masses of people. In this article, we shall discuss some of the special challenges that India faces and the different approaches to tackling them that have been mooted in the public arena.

Even in western social democracies, the large social protection programmes for workers are suffering from stresses and strains, particularly from the point of view of fiscal stringency, anxieties of global competitiveness and shifts in political attitudes towards immigrant recipients of benefits. In India where inequality and mass poverty are large, there are doubts about the fiscal feasibility of even the barest minimum programmes and about the large-scale wastes and thefts such programmes often involve. In addition, the vast informal sector (larger than in most major developing countries: even outside agriculture more than 80% of Indian workers work informally) implies special difficulties and costs of administering such programmes.

RIGHTS-BASED APPROACH

In the discussion, there have been different approaches to the question of how to tackle social protection. A very popular approach these days is to couch it in terms of 'rights' (to food, education, information, jobs, etc), and there is a great deal of commendable activism on this front, and already some achievements to show, particularly in the landmark legislations on the right to information and to work on public works projects (though their implementation in many states are as yet rather slow and feeble, and facing a good deal of resistance from bureaucrats, contractors, etc). This approach can, at the minimum, serve to raise consciousness among the poor and vulnerable about their entitlements, a sense that they are not mere supplicants to the politicians or bureaucrats, that if the latter fail there is access to courts to enforce these rights, and public interest litigation and court injunctions on these matters have attracted a great deal of attention.

But at the same time one should recognise some limits to this rights-based approach. If the delivery structure for implementing some of these rights remains as weak and corrupt as it is now, mere promulgation of rights will remain hollow and will, after a point, generate a great deal of cynicism. The Indian public arena is already littered with hundreds of unenforced or spasmodically enforced court injunctions, and there is some danger of the proliferating judicial activism in stretching the interpretation of the constitutional 'right to life' ending up, for all its good intentions, in undermining the credibility and legitimacy of the judiciary itself.

For example, if the right to food is exerted with no consideration of the efficiency and cost-effectiveness of the ways of implementing it (like the current public distribution system (PDS) which in many states is an enormous project of theft and wastage—a rough estimate is that less than a quarter of the subsidised food grains reaches the poor), it is an unwarranted and unfair burden on taxpayers who fund the galloping costs. In any case, the programme as currently administered is weakest in the poorest regions that need it most. Food stamps that have been advocated from time to time will reduce some of the wastage and theft in the storage and distribution by public agencies, but will not eliminate the problems of (a) fraud rampant in non-universal means-tested targeting like that to below-poverty-line (BPL) people, and (b) the development of secondary markets where merchants buy up the stamps in exchange of some (smaller) cash—in which case you might as well directly give people cash rather than stamps. The recent Right to Education Act (2009) does very little for the poor quality—and quantity—of education services actually provided in government schools (that drive children to private schools even though teachers there are by and large less qualified and less well-paid) or about the negligence with which the new poor students foisted on the private schools are likely to be treated without a proper quality evaluation of schools in place, or the remedial education that the poor-performing children (at private or government schools) and the school dropouts desperately need.

The current National Rural Employment Guarantee Act (NREGA), the largest of its kind anywhere in the world, for all its flaws (which would have been far less if a regular and institutionalised system of independent social audits were in place—only Andhra Pradesh government has institutionalised them), provides a possible fall-back option for many able bodied rural adults for working on mostly construction projects for a period of 100 days every year (though this limit of 100 days and timely payment of wages have so far been reached only in very few areas). This may have already exerted some positive indirect effects on the rural wage earned by the poorest people.

JOB VS ECONOMIC SECURITY

This is, of course, quite different from the right to a job often demanded by organised workers in the formal sector. The right to a job, if narrowly interpreted as the security on a given job, can considerably distort the labour market, if it freezes the ability of the employer (public or private) to adjust to changing conditions in technology or market, thus hurting the whole economy, and the job prospects of less privileged workers. It is very important to distinguish between economic security and job security. A worker should have the right to expect from society general economic security, but not security on a given job.

My own empirical judgement, however, is that stringent labour laws that are aimed at ensuring job security in large industrial firms may not be the most important constraint on Indian industrial growth; other constraints like infrastructure, credit and marketing may be more important in many cases, but that they constitute a constraint cannot be denied. There is ultimately no alternative to a package deal between employers and organised workers: allowing more flexibility in hiring and firing has to be combined with a reasonable scheme of unemployment compensation or adjustment assistance, from a earmarked fund to which employers and employees should both contribute. No Indian politician has yet gathered the courage or imagination to come up with such a package deal.

The distinction between economic security and security of a particular job (usually in the formal sector) also brings to the foreground a particular conflict among workers which organised trade unions would rather ignore. It is well-known that social democracy in Western Europe came out of a historic compromise between capital and labour (the latter gets socially protected and a reasonable share of the economic pie, and in return gives up its democratic power of expropriating the former, so that it can carry on its innovations that expand the pie).

In India where the informal sector is massive, social democracy may require an additional implicit compromise in the labour market, between formal and informal workers— since in many ways their interests may be in conflict (one example is that stringent job protection of formal workers may be at the expense of the potential expansion of job possibilities for informal workers; another example is that the general strikes and bandhs frequently called by formal sector unions as part of their organisational muscle-flexing paralyse city life and rob the daily informal workers and street vendors of their subsistence). Besides, the strongest organised workers are those in the public sector services, and it is their corrupt and callous service non-delivery which the poor informal workers as potential recipients have to face every day.

In general, one should not look at the social protection rights in abstraction from costs (direct and indirect), delivery mechanisms or even their political constituency. Well-designed, well-administered, cost effective programmes of implementing some basic rights generate more political support even among those who are paying for them. One should, of course, mention here that one positive implication of the rights approach is that of universal principles and standards, which in some cases may help better administration. For example, it has been pointed out that the PDS for food generates less malfeasance when it is universal (as in Tamil Nadu and Chhattisgarh); as we have indicated before, when some people are excluded under a targeted system of delivery, it leads to dual markets and more incentives and opportunities for fraud, apart from eroding its larger political support base.

UNIVERSAL BASIC INCOME

On the universalistic principle of social protection, one of the cleanest and least incentive-disruptive ideas, both ethically and economically compelling, is that of Universal Basic Income (UBI), under which everybody, rich or poor, gets an unconditional annual (or periodic) income supplement. This is an old idea, originally inspired by some European 'utopian socialists' in the 19th century, tried unsuccessfully in McGovern's 1968 presidential campaign in the US in the form of a proposed 'demogrant', currently supported by some

Green Parties in Europe, and actually implemented in non-socialist resource-rich Alaska since 1999 (in the form of an annual Permanent Fund Dividend). In the West, the discussion in opposition to the idea usually centres around the encouragement this may give to idleness and dependency and the 'unfairness' of a hand-out to the rich as well.

I think we need to worry less about idleness in a country where the overwhelming majority of the people are extremely poor and overworked. Giving to the rich as well may be found administratively tolerable by many who know the formidable problems of monitoring and corruption in India in trying to target it only to the poor. The main question is: if we want it to be universal, can we afford it? Of course, the answer depends on the amount to be given out, if it will be a replacement for the existing transfer programmes which have a lot of wastage and misappropriation, how the problem of misappropriation of the basic income supplement will be handled, etc. Let us make some back-of-the envelope calculations.

Suppose in a country of 1.2 billion people, we want to give out every year Rs 5,000 to each family (assumed to have five members). This amounts to Rs 1,20,000 crore (not counting administrative costs, which need not be large, with electronic help). Let us assume, for the time being, that with the forthcoming installation of the electronic Unique Identification (UID) system, the administrative costs of this unconditional transfer programme will be minimal. Let us now compare this sum of Rs 1,20,000 crore with some benchmark figures. The total estimates of how much is currently spent by the government on all the anti-poverty programmes together easily exceed this amount. What is even more important is that this amount is much less than the total subsidies the government gives out to the relatively rich every year. We do not have iron-clad estimates of the latter. The National Institute of Public Finance and Policy has from time to time estimated the total amount of subsidies (implicit as well as explicit) given out by the central and the state governments.

This comes to about 14% of GDP every year. These subsidies are classified into 'merit' and 'non-merit' subsidies.

Without going into the intricacies of the definitions, let us say, very roughly, that the non-merit subsidies mostly go to the relatively rich. Of the 14% of GDP in total subsidies, roughly two-thirds have been estimated to be non-merit subsidies: that comes to about 9% of GDP. Let us make a conservative estimate and bring this figure down to 6% of GDP as going to the relatively rich. In 2009-10, the annual GDP of India was about Rs 45,00,000 crore (at 2004-05 prices); 6% of this comes to Rs 2,70,000 crore. So what the government pays out as subsidies every year to the relatively rich is more than double the amount it will need to pay out a basic income supplement of Rs 5,000 to each family, rich or poor.

In other words, if one can somehow halve the existing subsidies to the relatively rich, that will be more than enough to cover the basic income supplement for everybody. And if this replaces some of the existing dysfunctional programmes (like PDS) or not very effective cash transfer programmes (like the Swarnajayanti Gram Swarojgar Yojana or the Indira Awas Yojana), the income supplement can be even larger (or the reduction in the subsidies to the rich may be smaller). All this is based on a very rough and ready calculation and one should not take the estimates too seriously, but it gives us some sense of proportion.

But are the possibilities of misappropriation that afflict most social protection programmes in India seriously lower with the basic income supplement idea fortified with UID? If the money is electronically deposited in an account (at a nearby post office or bank) from which withdrawals require biometric identification, and no means-testing or rich-poor classification is necessary, many of the current problems of fraud and corruption and manipulation of BPL category are likely to diminish considerably. Yet one cannot rule out possibilities of clerks who would issue the withdrawn money demanding bribes, or local musclemen regularly extorting some of the cash from the defenceless recipient (like thieves in many countries taking their victims to the ATM machines and forcing withdrawals). Of course, when PDS gives a poor man subsidised food that can also be robbed and sold in the market, but I suppose the lure of direct cash may be stronger for the criminals. Similarly, chances of alcoholics and drug addict recipients blowing the cash are a problem that worries many critics of such programmes.

Of course, there are two kinds of reaction to this. One kind is the libertarian one, saying that we should let people decide how they want to spend the money, bearing the consequences of their decision is part of the responsibility that every individual has to take, etc. The other is the soft-paternalistic kind, trying to minimise the problem by handing over the money to the usually more responsible female adult in the household, devising all kinds of good-specific vouchers, etc. But there are problems of intra-household dynamics. In a country where women and children are among the most deprived in the usual way a household is run, and child and maternal mortality and malnutrition are among the worst in the world, concerns about how unequally the unconditional cash transfer is spent by the family are to be expected and the matter may not be left simply to the mercy of individual responsibility.

More importantly, just handing over more money to the poor resolves only part (the financial part) of the social protection they need. As petty producers they also need other kinds of assistance (knowledge, skills, marketing connections, etc) or as patients they need information about doctor quality, health practices, nutrition and sanitation, and so on. In the urban slums where the rural kin group support structures are weaker, social protection has also to involve active social support structures against violence, drugs, family breakdowns, juvenile delinquency, etc.

CONDITIONAL CASH TRANSFERS

In any case, it is probably highly unrealistic to expect that the relatively rich in India will easily give up on much of the subsidies they enjoy or that the vested interests that have accumulated around long-standing wasteful programmes like PDS will allow anything more than moderate tinkering. So proposals like unconditional cash transfers or Universal Basic Income supplements are unlikely to fly in the politics of the foreseeable future, as the question of 'can we afford such programmes?' will remain under those political constraints, even though, as we have seen, in principle it is resolvable. New programmes of social protection with a great deal of targeting (with lower costs but also more leakages) and some additional garnering of resources are more likely to be implemented. One class of such programmes is that of conditional cash transfers, with the added weapon of UID. In some sense, the NREGA is one such programme, of cash conditional on work, with self-targeting saving some administrative costs and leakage as the non-poor will not usually want to work on such manual, often back-breaking, construction works. UID may reduce a great deal of current leakage in the form of false muster rolls of workers. In the delivery of social services, nothing on the scale of Oportunidades in Mexico or Bolsa Familia in Brazil has yet been attempted in India. Most of the conditional cash transfer programmes for these services in India have been relatively small and aimed at ensuring the survival of girl children (and their mothers at the time of birth), and their continued education in schools and in raising their age at marriage. We do not yet have enough rigorous evaluation of these programmes.

In general, the main presumption of conditional transfer programmes is somewhat paternalistic: left to themselves the poor do not exert enough effort in sending their children to school, health clinics, immunisation centres, etc. So transfer programmes try to induce them with contingent transfers. There is a large administrative cost in monitoring and enforcing the stipulated conditions. In any case, such demand-sided interventions (inducing the poor to demand the services) do not solve the supply-side problems which are severe in India: not enough schools or health clinics, facilities, quality teachers or doctors, teacher and doctor absenteeism, etc. It will require some time for the supplies (private as well as public) of these services to be induced by increased demand and a great deal of regulations to ensure minimum quality. Of course, on the supply side, our bureaucracy is often not mindful of (or interested in) the fact that the government may be the financier but need not be the actual supplier and can work out all kinds of innovative solutions. For example, it can finance the education services but outsource some of them (as in the case of charter schools in the US); just as in the case of PDS, the Food Corporation of India can outsource its warehousing to private companies, instead of letting its procured grains rot outside (about one quarter of the total in late 2010 and early 2011) for lack of public warehousing space.

GOVERNANCE AND SOCIAL SERVICES

The main bottleneck in the delivery of social services in India is, of course, in the governance mechanism and the incentive systems in operation. There are very few performance incentives in the reward structure for officials. Promotion is largely seniority-based. Frequent transfers, sometimes arbitrarily determined by the political bosses, discourage the development of any stake in any particular locality of service. Bad performance is very seldom punished; in any case, the measurement of performance is 'noisy' particularly when the quality of service is necessarily multidimensional. This promotes a rampant culture of impunity. The schoolteachers, doctors and nurses, for example, are not punished for the dereliction of their duties, their salaries and promotions are decided from above, not by the local people who bear the brunt.

This obviously suggests the need for decentralisation and accountability downwards. In fact, there is some evidence that in some cases (eg, in Nagaland) where even a very small fraction of the teachers' salary was paid by the local panchayat, it immediately led to a significant improvement in services. But in most parts of India, while local elections are now regularly held, effective decentralisation is missing, on account of a severe dearth of devolved funds or delegated power or appropriate professional personnel. Local elections are usually fought on supra-local issues, and more often than not the state-level politicians and bureaucrats hijack the process of mandated devolution. Such hijacking is made easier by the lack of inner-party democracy in almost all political parties, so that local political leaders are at the mercy of the higher-tier leadership. It has not been widely recognised in India how the lack of inner-party democracy, apart from making political parties structurally undemocratic, has the side effect of corroding the vitals of local democracy in India.

HEALTH SERVICES

The other incentive and structural problems in governance in social services may be illustrated from the health sector (qualitatively some similar issues arise also in education or nutrition programmes). At the moment, healthcare in India is primarily private (and largely unregulated). Household survey data suggest that 85% of all visits for healthcare in rural areas, even by the poorest people, are to private practitioners. While the poor quality of service in public clinics and hospitals (and absenteeism by nurses and doctors) often drive patients to private doctors (some of them quacks or crooks), in some cases even when the public services are available, the patients prefer going to private medical practitioners who more readily oblige them with unnecessary antibiotics and steroids.

The public health delivery system is afflicted by poor provider incentives, coupled with low accountability to the patients. The medical personnel are paid a fixed salary independent of the number of patients or of their visits, so they have no economic incentive to serve them in the public clinic (they have all the incentive to ask patients to come to their private chambers for paid service and send them for unnecessary diagnostic tests at labs in which they have a monetary interest). The poor have very little organised 'voice' in sanctioning the errant provider. They are assertive in elections, but even a local election is a blunt instrument of sanction for any particular service: electoral platforms are multidimensional where specific grievances about any particular public service provider get diluted, often by larger state-wide issues. In addition, compared to curative medical services, the Indian system is particularly deficient in systematic planning and delivery of preventive public health services or sustained programmes of large-scale disease control (the public health administration in Tamil Nadu, I understand, is a major exception). One of the cost-viability problems for any public health insurance service for the poor in India (like the as yet fledgling programme—Rashtriya Swasthya Bima Yojana—that is supposed to cover up to Rs 30,000 for only hospitalisation-related expenses for BPL families) is that the poor in most cases go for hospitalisation with illnesses (like diarrhoea or typhoid or malaria) which could be prevented by basic public health programmes like provision of clean drinking water, sanitation, spraying, etc. Thus the deficiencies of public health administration in India in carrying out its primary duties make healthcare insurance so costly.

Outside of government or private provision of health services, there can be other alternatives. Several NGOs in India, as part of their development programmes, have initiated community health insurance schemes for poor people, often linking up with an insurer (with a larger risk pool) and purchasing healthcare from an external provider. Self-Employed Women's Association in Gujarat is an important example of organising community health insurance for its members and their families in this way. This and other similar models need to be studied and replicated in a much larger scale in worker associations and cooperatives in India, particularly in the informal sector. In the history of

German social welfare programmes, worker associations played a leading role. In India, where the informal sector is much larger, small-scale associations need to be mobilised for social insurance, the NGOs can play a mediating role with insurers and help processing payments of premium (apart from identifying beneficiaries and giving them the requisite information), and the government can introduce some provider accreditation systems to help the choice of providers.

CONCLUSION

In conclusion, while the discussion on social democracy in western countries often puts the emphasis on its high costs (particularly in view of the austerities necessitated by intense global competition) and issues of incentives for work and enterprise, in India high inequality, massive poverty and a vast informal sector make the challenge of implementing social democracy extremely daunting as much as it is highly imperative. The particular governance issues in India, with inept, corrupt and unmotivated public officials in charge of the delivery system, make the mobilisation of social groups and community organisations and various participatory processes all the more important. But there is a more fundamental issue here that involves the interaction of the productive system and the political culture. As we have mentioned before, European social democracy is the outcome of a class compromise and a social pact: the workers who are electorally powerful enough to expropriate the capitalists and end the capitalist system have chosen not to do so, they have figured out that capitalism is the only viable way left for adequately expanding the pie, so they are prepared to bear some cost ('exploitation') and let the capitalists have a reasonable share of that pie which induces the latter to keep at their efforts at bringing about dynamic innovations. I am not sure if the Indian electorate has yet been confronted with this social pact, and if so confronted how they will react.

After the demise of the short-lived Swatantra Party, India has not had a full-scale pro-business conservative party; even the right wing parties are largely populist on many economic issues when they go to the electorate. In spite of the great flowering of entrepreneurial energies in recent years throughout the country, I believe there is a strong anti-capitalist (particularly anti-big-capital) streak in Indian political culture. This is not surprising in a country where small people (small and middle peasants, self-employed artisans and shopkeepers, bazaar merchants and petty middlemen, clerks, schoolteachers and service workers) constitute an overwhelming majority of the population, and their ranks are swelled by the inexorable demographic pressure and by the traditional inheritance practices involving subdivision of property. There is a deep suspicion of market competition whereby the larger economic interests, often utilising their advantages of economies of scale, deeper pockets and better political connections, can devour the small. Gandhi had given sensitive and eloquent expression to this anti-market, anti-big-capital, small-is-beautiful populism and mobilised it in the freedom movement against the British. In recent decades, those bearing the legacy of the Gandhian moral critique of market expansion and competition have joined forces with those espousing the left critique of capitalist exploitation of workers, peasants, and other small people and their rights over natural resources, in building active grass roots movements in parts of the country for the protection of the environment and of the traditional livelihood of the indigenous people, against the depredations of the capitalist oligarchy. Even though the private corporate sector is thriving in India and in some sense its 'hegemony' looks more pervasive today than before, it is involved in the work life of too few people (as it directly employs not more than 2% of the Indian work force), and it is not clear that the electorate is still ready to accept the class compromise like the one behind the social democracy enterprise in the West.

On the other hand, the populist opposition, for all their strength in numbers, have not yet succeeded in pointing to any viable, incentive-compatible (ie, not entirely dependent on revolutionary or moral zeal for sustenance), systemic economic alternative, outside the esoteric confines of their wishful thinking or utopian anarcho-communitarianism. The passionate intensity of their negative critique of capitalism is not matched by a convincing demonstration of a sustained positive alternative system on a scale large enough to generate the necessary surplus. Until this tension is resolved, the social democracy project in India will remain somewhat tentative. Under the circumstances, the great danger for the social-democratic striving is that it may dissipate itself in various costly and in the long run harmful populist schemes, utilised by the political process for narrow patronage distribution goals.

Reflections on
Indian Political Economy

Economic & Political Weekly, 2 May 2015

Over the 30 years since *The Political Economy of Development in India* (OUP, 1984, 1998) was published, I have noticed a remarkable asymmetry in its reception among mainstream economists and others. The book has received nothing but benign neglect from the former group. I am pretty sure most of my colleagues in the major Economics Departments in the United States (US) have never heard of this book, even though many of them may be aware of my more technical articles in journals. Looking back I have sometimes thought that maybe it would have attracted more attention of economists if I had published in the book the background theoretical notes I had for a couple of its main messages.

One such message was about the difficulty of organising collective action towards long-term public investment in infrastructure, a key ingredient of economic growth, in a country where even the elite is fragmented and finds it difficult to get its act together in doing something that would have benefited most of its members. With this failure of collective action, the public surplus is often frittered away in short-term subsidies and handouts. Since writing the 1984 book I have elsewhere (Bardhan, 2005) elaborated on my theoretical ideas on the adverse effect of social heterogeneity and inequality on collective action not just on matters of macroeconomic growth but also in the microeconomic issues of management of local commons. The other message, enunciated in the last chapter of the book, for which I had some unpublished theoretical notes, was how the same elite fragmentation that acts as a constraint on economic growth can work as a safeguard for the resilience of democracy in India, where the divided groups may agree on the procedures of democracy as a means of keeping one another within some bounds of moderation in their transactional negotiations.[1]

COLLECTIVE ACTION ISSUE

This article first discusses the collective action issue for long-term growth that I had identified more than three decades back and which remains acute even today in India. It then moves onto a discussion of a few of the structural issues not considered in the 1984 book that have become prominent in recent years.

The economic growth fundamentals for India are now potentially quite strong (stronger than it seemed in 1984):

- Domestic saving and investment rates are relatively high for a poor country.
- After the opening of the Indian economy, the alacrity with which a part of the hitherto protected Indian business adapted to the demands of global competition and thrived suggests a remarkable adaptability.
- Vigorous entrepreneurial spirit in all corners of the economy, rejuvenated by the infusion of business entries from hitherto subordinate castes and regional capitalists.
- The majority of the population is quite young, with the potential of a large and productive young workforce.
- With better transport and communication (particularly with the remarkably fast spread of mobile phones), connectivity is increasing in a way that is likely to speed up enhancement of productivity.

But there are major structural and institutional problems blocking the full realisation of these strong growth fundamentals:

(a) The physical infrastructure (roads, electricity, ports, railways, etc) is weak. Public budgets laden with heavy subsidies, salaries and debt servicing have very little left for infrastructure investment, leading to increasing frequency of public-private partnerships on infrastructure. But these have often been saddled with problems of mismanagement, very high debt–equity ratios, opportunistic renegotiation, non-transparent regulations and corruption. In addition, caught in the crossfire between corporate lobbies on the one hand and social activists and judiciary on the other, official land and environmental clearances for infrastructure projects have become extremely slow, non-transparent or erratic (lurching from one side to the other) in recent years.

(b) Secondary education is a minimum qualification for many good non-farm jobs, and yet the children from poor families overwhelmingly drop out before entering or completing secondary schools, on account of economic and, particularly in the case of girls, also social compulsions.

(c) The average quality of school and college education is not sufficient for employable skills for many, even for some manual, jobs. The provisions for vocational training and skill formation along with connections with potential employers, particularly for rural youth, are extremely deficient. In a so-called 'labour-surplus' country, there is now a serious shortage of employable labour in factories and other enterprises.

(d) Despite all the economic growth of recent years, a major social and organisational failure, almost at a disastrous level, over many decades has been in matters of public health and sanitation, where India lags behind even some African countries.[2] Poor public health and sanitation continue to keep the Indian disease burden high and the productivity of workers low.

(e) Environmental degradation has been a major drag on net economic growth. It has been reported in the 2014 United Nations Development Programme's (UNDP) Human Development Report that the annual depletion in natural resources (depreciation of 'natural' capital) in India as proportion of national income (conventionally measured) is nearing 5% per year (not very different from the growth rate in national income in recent years), compared to 3.6% for Brazil and 0.1% for Costa Rica.[3] It has been assessed by the World Health Organization that of the 20 most air-polluted cities in the world, 13 are in India. (Indoor and outdoor) air pollution kills an estimated 1.6 million people every year.

GOVERNANCE INEFFECTIVENESS

All of the above—infrastructure, education, public health and sanitation, environment—involve the governance effectiveness issue with respect to delivery of key public goods and services, which is rather low in India, and, of course, varies a great deal between different states in India (Mundle et al, 2012).

Governance ineffectiveness is often regarded as a lack of state capacity, that many point to as India's major failing. While it is true that the bureaucracy is often inept or corrupt or simply truant, it is equally important to keep in mind that state capacity is sometimes weak not necessarily because of a dearth of capable people but because of a systemic impasse. Extraordinary state capacity may be observed in some episodic matters, for example, in organising the complex logistics of the world's largest elections, the world's second largest census, and some of the world's largest religious festivals. But extraordinarily poor state capacity is displayed in, for example, some regular essential activities like cost-effective pricing and distribution of electricity—the key input for the economy.

There exist regular under-recovery of costs, erratic supply and anaemic investment in electricity, caused not so much by an inherent lack of administrative capacity, but more by factors relating to complicity in a sinister political nexus, populist pressures and outright theft. Similarly, much of the police and bureaucracy are highly politicised and often deliberately incapacitated. Corruption in India is often more dysfunctional, than say in the more politically centralised countries of East Asia, primarily because it is fragmented, with no encompassing centralising entity, internalising the distortions ('negative externalities') of each act of corruption.[4]

The apparent lack of state capacity may be more a symptom of the underlying difficulty of organising collective action (or collectively working out a 'social pact') in India, a problem exacerbated by its large heterogeneous population, fragmented polity and extreme social and economic inequality. In such a context, commitments on the part of the state are often not credible, and anticipating that different interest and identity groups settle for short-run patronage and subsidies. This brings me back to the main theme of difficulty of collective action emphasised in the 1984 book.

Since 1984 the population has increased considerably both in size and the diversity of now-assertive groups. The polity is more fragmented (even in the most recent, unusually aggregative and presidential, national election signs of high political fragmentation remain—36 political parties with at least one seat in the Parliament; the vote share of regional parties still remaining almost half, etc). While social inequality may be on a slow decline, economic inequality has almost certainly increased.

Thus, by and large, the consequent problems for collective action may have become more severe, in spite of centralisation of power under the new regime.

FOUR STRUCTURAL ISSUES

Let me now move to the second part of this article, by pointing briefly to at least four types of structural issues, not considered in the 1984 book, where there are significant unresolved tensions that the Indian political economy will have to grapple with in the coming years.

(a) There is a brewing 'legitimisation crisis' of capitalism in India for many sections of the people on account of
    (1) rising inequality of wealth,
    (2) the flourishing of 'crony' capitalism (exemplified by the so-called Gujarat model of development),
    (3) the displacements and dispossession of common people from their land and degradation of their environment, and
    (4) deterioration in the supply of basic public services (water, safety, etc) in the burgeoning cities and towns, while the rich arrange for private access to these services.

In reaction, quite often politicians try to placate the citizen with short-run populist measures. But the legitimisation issue has also induced over the last couple of decades, vigorous social movements and pressures for the recognition of various kinds of citizen rights and accountability institutions. (The Left, or whatever is left of the Left in party politics, has so far given mostly rhetorical support to these movements, without putting its organisational muscle into them.)

These movements, however, have occasionally ended up stalling industrial progress—in collaboration with judicial activism they have made mining, infrastructural and environment clearances sometimes very difficult, slowing industrial growth.

The debates all around have become polarised on this matter, and political decisions seem to lurch from one end to the other—under the United Progressive Alliance (UPA) in the early years the rights movement flourished, but in the last two years or so, under UPA as well as the National Democratic Alliance (NDA) governments, the pendulum has swung again in favour of corporate lobbies.

Since the social movements have not yet taken the form of mass political organisations, it has been relatively easy for business-friendly governments to bypass or dilute earlier welfarist legislative actions in actual implementation. To negotiate some kind of political balance in this tug of war between competing interests will be complex and time-consuming, and the Indian polity will go on vacillating on these issues. And following usual political practice, parties in opposition will agitate against policies they themselves supported while in power.

The mainly elite-led but thriving nongovernmental organisations and other voluntary organisations act often as strident single-interest lobbies, making compromise difficult. In this respect, they are poor substitutes for large multifarious political parties. But with the decay of inner-party democracy in all the parties, political parties no longer act as a forum for deliberation and transactional negotiations between contending interest groups within the party on controversial policy issues, where there are always trade-offs which could be negotiated.

(b) More than citizen rights and welfare, the young people who are the majority of 'aspirational' India seem to be demanding jobs. Over the next decade or so this can be a major source of political turmoil, particularly because over many decades job growth in India has been very sluggish. Every month there are about a million new entries into the nonfarm labour force, but outside the construction sector, the growth elasticity of job creation so far has been extremely low. Most recent economic success stories in India have been in relatively skill-intensive or capital-intensive industries (software, pharmaceuticals, vehicles, auto parts, etc).

There are several constraints on large-scale labour-intensive industrialisation in India—infrastructure, skill formation, credit, regulatory environment, contract enforcement problems, red tape and inspector raj, etc. We do not yet have good statistical decomposition exercises on the net impact of these various factors on job creation or lack of it.

The business press and some liberal economists habitually put much of the blame on trade unions, but they overlook the fact that trade unions (particularly of unskilled workers) are now substantially weaker than before, partly on account of forces of technology, and increased capital mobility both across countries and across states in India.

Even in the organised sector, more than one-third of workers are now 'contract labourers' without security or benefits, sometimes working side by side with regular workers.

(c) Even when jobs are created, there is a major regional discrepancy between job demand and supply, which may turn the so-called demographic dividend from large numbers of young people into a ticking time bomb in parts of the country. For demographic reasons these young people are more in the large populous states of North India (where poor governance and infrastructural deficiency limit job growth as well as delivery of welfare services). But jobs, when created, are more in states in West and South India. Interstate migration can be a partial relief but, given the staggering numbers, it cannot be a solution if one wants to avoid large costs of dislocation and nativist unrest.

The current government and the Fourteenth Finance Commission seem to be encouraging more devolution of finance and responsibility to the states. With large initial differences in state capacity and infrastructural deficit, this is likely to accentuate regional inequality and discontent. With capital being much more mobile across states than unskilled labour, many states are likely to compete in giving concessions to capital while indulging in populist measures for the poor.

(d) Tension between rentier and entrepreneurial capitalism: There are three major sources of rent:

(1) Traded natural resource intensive goods (like minerals). In the last decade, the mining mafia had its way, but with global recession and slowing down of the Chinese economy, this source of rental income is a bit weaker now.

(2) Non-traded natural resource-intensive goods and services (like land and real estate).

(3) Political rent in other activities (following from collusion between politicians/bureaucrats and connected sets of favoured businessmen).

Even after liberalisation, capital crucially depends on various kinds of regulatory discretion of officials as well as loans from public banks—large corporate defaulters on the latter have recently been described by the Reserve Bank of India Governor as 'freeloaders'.

There is hardly any major state or political party in India which has not been corrupted by land and real estate interests. As the economy grows and land prices in a densely populated country gallop, this is unlikely to diminish in importance. (There is some evidence that land price rise in India in recent years has been one of the highest in the world, Chakraborty, 2013.)

POLITICAL RENTS

On political rent, there are, of course, built-in checks in economic competition (if scale economies are not large barriers to entry), particularly from abroad, and the political competition of democracy. Though the domestic non-traded part is large, the Indian economy is now sufficiently globally integrated for the economic check to be quite significant in many sectors. There is, however, not much evidence that the dominance of incumbent firms has declined in the Indian industrial sector even after economic liberalisation (Alfaro & Chari, 2013). On political competition, the barriers to political entry are getting stiffer, as elections become inordinately expensive and all campaigning politicians are increasingly dependent on scarce, often illicit, financial and organisational resources.

The impact of rentier capitalism on politics is to encourage oligarchic forces. In US history, the 'robber barons' of the 19th century were partially checked by the institutions created by the politics of the 'progressive era'. Much will depend on if or how a sufficient number of accountability institutions develop in India. Our elections are vigorous but our democracy is enormously flawed in terms of various kinds of accountability failures, particularly at the local level.

It is this uphill democratic struggle that will shape the future of Indian political economy.

NOTES

1 For a recent game-theoretic model of intra-elite conflicts and democracy on broadly related lines, see Ghosal & Eugenio, 2009.
2 According to the 2014 *Human Development Report* of the UNDP, the deaths of children under age five due to unsafe water, unimproved sanitation or poor hygiene per hundred thousand children numbered 316 in India in 2004, whereas they were 255 in Sudan, 256 in Zimbabwe and 286 in Gambia.
3 A recent book edited by Mani (2014) estimates that in 2009 the cost of environmental degradation in India came to 5.7% of GDP.
4 For an analytical discussion of this issue, see Bardhan, 2005, Chapter 8.

REFERENCES

Alfaro, L & A Chari, *Deregulation, Misallocation and Size: Evidence from India*, NBER Working Paper No 18650, 2013

Bardhan, P, *The Political Economy of Development in India*, Oxford and New York: Basil Blackwell, 1984, 1998

Bardhan, P, *Scarcity, Conflicts and Cooperation*, Cambridge, MA: MIT Press, 2005

Chakraborty, S, *The Price of Land*, New Delhi: Oxford University Press, 2013

Ghosal, S & P Eugenio, 'Democracy, Collective Action and Intra-Elite Conflict', *Journal of Public Economics*, 93(9-10), 2009, pp.1078-89

Mani, M (ed.), *Greening India's Growth: Costs, Valuations and Trade-offs*, London: Routledge, 2014

Mundle, S, P Chakraborty, S Chowdhury & S Sikdar, 'The Quality of Governance: How Have Indian States Performed?', *Economic & Political Weekly*, 47(49), 2012

Challenges for
Two of the Largest Democracies

3 Quarks Daily, 18 March 2019

In the next couple of months two of the largest democracies in the world—India and Indonesia—will have their national elections. At a time when democracy is under considerable pressure everywhere, the electoral and general democratic outcome in these two countries containing in total more than one and a half billion people (more than one and a half times the population in democratic West plus Japan and Australia) will be closely observed.

Let's start with India. Many Indians, while preening about their country being the largest democracy, are often in denial about how threadbare the quality of that democracy actually has been, particularly in recent years. Indian elections are vigorous (barring some occasional complaints about intimidations and irregularities) and largely competitive (the Indian electorate is usually more anti-incumbent than, say, the American). But other essential aspects of democracy—respect for basic civic and human rights and established procedures of accountability in day-to-day governance—are quite weak. (I don't like the oxymoronic term 'illiberal democracy', used by many people—from Fareed Zakaria to Viktor Orban—as this ignores those essential aspects of democracy.)

In India (as in Indonesia) democracy is often mis-identified with a kind of crude majoritarianism. The Hindu nationalists who currently rule India often trample on minority rights with shameless impunity. They have created an atmosphere of hateful violence and intimidation against dissidents and minorities, where freedom of expression by artists, writers, scholars, journalists and others is routinely violated. Supposed 'group rights' trump individual rights: individual freedom of expression has very little chance if some group claims to take offence. Courts sometimes take redemptive action, usually with great delay, but meanwhile the damage is done in intimidating large numbers of people.

Several universities are currently under assault (both by ruling party goons and politicians), and school textbooks in a few states are seriously distorting history. The appointment of a bigoted Hindu-militant monk as the Chief Minister of India's largest state, Uttar Pradesh, was a bit like the Republican Party in the US appointing the Grand Wizard of Ku Klux Klan as, say, the Governor of Texas. (The state now tops in incidents of hate crimes in India, according to the latest report from Amnesty International.) Encouraged by such leaders roving groups in North India are terrorising people in the name of cow protection. These cow-worshippers are oblivious how their coercive interference with cattle trade and transport is wreaking havoc on the larger cattle and farm economy, with huge numbers of stray and aged cattle loose in the countryside.

Many voluntary groups (NGOs) in the business of critical monitoring of the implementation of public policies are regularly harassed and frightened by hostile action from government agencies—one tool of harassment is the arbitrary application of the FCRA, Foreign Contribution Regulation Act (from which, by the way, all political parties are exempt). In India the political parties are neither public entities (GOs) to which the Right to Information Act, 2005 (RTI) should apply, nor NGOs to which the FCRA is to apply, and meanwhile they enjoy tax exemption.

In the Social Hostilities Index, brought out by the Pew Research Center for 198 countries, at the end of 2016 India was among the 8 worst (the index labeled 'Very High') countries (Indonesia was in the 'High' group). In the World Press Freedom Index, brought out by Reporters without Borders, in 2017-18 India's rank among 180 countries was 138 (Indonesia's was 124, slightly better). In the Rule of Law Index brought out by the World Justice Project for 113 countries, in 2017-18 India's rank was 62 (tied with Indonesia). In the Report of the Economist Intelligence Unit on the State of Democracy in the World for 2018, both India and Indonesia are in the category of 'flawed', not full, democracy; out of 167 countries India's rank is 41, worse than Latvia, Taiwan or Botswana (Indonesia's is even worse at 65)—the rank for both India and Indonesia having sharply declined compared to 2014. In general, there is not much to be proud of in these indices for the world's largest democracy.

Of course, the Indian government and business economists show off India's high growth rates (higher than those in other major developing countries, including Indonesia). The growth rate numbers (with some doubts occasionally arising from mismatch with figures about credit or investment or crude alternative measures of economic activity) and those about fiscal deficits (served with a bit of creative accounting) are primarily for the consumption of credit rating agencies and foreign investors. At election time, the ruling party politicians are shrewd enough to realise that high growth rates (particularly when they have not created commensurate numbers of good jobs for the bulging population of youths) do not cut much ice with the restive electorate. So they go for widely publicised sops like loan waivers and income support for (the currently distressed) farmers and other handouts.

The current government has no doubt had some laudable economic achievements in providing some measure of financial inclusion, roads, housing, sanitation, gas for cooking fuel, etc for the poor, and somewhat less cumbersome regulations, streamlining of value-added taxes (though clumsily implemented) and insolvency procedures for business. But actual progress in much of these has not matched the constant barrage of official hype, and the Indian economy, particularly in the vast informal sector, has barely recovered from the whimsical onslaught of demonetisation in November 2016 thought up by an ignorant but arrogant leadership and carried out by a confused and unprepared banking bureaucracy.

The government refuses to have any dialogue with most labour organisations in the country (except its own party-affiliated one) on the issues of so-called labour reform. On most social indicators, involving education and health, India's progress has been unimpressive even for its level of per capita income. In the Human Capital Index recently prepared by the World Bank, out of 157 countries India's rank is 115, even worse than poorer neighbours like Bangladesh and Nepal (Indonesia's rank is better, at 87). On balance, it is not clear how helpful the record of economic performance will be for the ruling party in the elections. When claims about the economy (with Modi as 'vikash-purush' or Mr Development) do not work, the ruling party has an ominous history of invoking religious symbols (like promising to build a Hindu temple on the rubble of a destroyed mosque) and strategically stoking communal suspicion and polarisation, or supercharged jingoism against a neighbouring Muslim country, all of which often helping the immediate electoral prospects of a majoritarian party.

In any case, the ruling party has four major advantages in the forthcoming elections:

(a) an effective demagogue in the Prime Minister with considerable oratorical and campaign skills;

(b) a ramshackle and disunited opposition at the national level with no defining positive narrative that can catch public imagination;

(c) a cadre-based army of volunteers which does the all-important last-mile electioneering for the ruling party; and

(d) a grossly lopsided advantage in funding for the increasingly expensive business of fighting elections—even of the legitimately raised large donations, the ruling party has mobilised an estimated 92% of them, not to speak of the large illegitimate or unaccounted donations.

Yet, as political scientists and psephologists will tell you, much will depend on the intricate arithmetic of caste and regional group alliances expediently forged by opposing sides and their fluidity in a bewilderingly diverse and vast country like India. In this the political centralisation of the ruling party is both an advantage (in keeping the organisation disciplined and focused) and a disadvantage (in riding roughshod over regional leaders and factions). Similarly, its upper-caste 'vote bank' is an advantage arising from its solid loyalty, but a possible liability in stitching alliances with the more numerous backward castes.

Whichever party wins the real long-term challenge for the Indian democratic polity is to stem the rot of its institutional foundations. The institutional decay hollowing out the shell of democracy started a few decades back, but under some rulers it has accelerated—in this respect the worst have been the regimes of Indira Gandhi and Narendra Modi. The executive overreach and abuse has dissipated the independence of police and bureaucracy (often used for short-run narrow partisan ends), with tax and investigative agencies blithely used for personal vendetta of leaders and for cynical stirring of, or keeping on slow boil, the anti-corruption investigations just for continual smearing of opposition politicians, not necessarily for their conclusive conviction, while cases against the ruling party politicians (or any new allies who are lured to their fold) are quietly dropped. Attempts to enfeeble the independence of regulatory bodies are quite common—even apex bodies like the Reserve Bank of India, the Supreme Court or the Election Commission of India have sometimes come under pressure—as are suppressions of unflattering data (and of statistical agencies that collect them). The centralisation of all power in the Prime Minister's Office, apart from making a mockery of the oft-repeated rhetoric of 'cooperative federalism' in the relation between the federal and state governments, has rendered the cabinet system of government of a parliamentary democracy largely ineffective. The legislature is used mainly for acclamation and hurried passing, without much discussion, of complex bills. The joint parliamentary committees that raise questions are starved of information and/or ignored.

Dissent is often branded as sedition and 'anti-national'— even though it is arguable that judged by the frequent violations of the Constitution in letter and spirit and of the civic nationalism that is based on constitutional values it is the ruling party and its affiliate organisations that are in some sense deeply anti-national. The Prime Minister who is quite effusive on all manners of things in his one-way tweets and radio chats falls eerily silent when inconvenient truths or atrocities by his party affiliates hit the news. While never hesitating in stressing his own muscular brand of leadership, he is strangely afraid to meet the press or any searching questions from journalists and legislators. He is open only to the part of the media that is fawning and to adulatory crowds. The media on their part are often beholden to the government for plum advertisements and to crony capitalists who own some of them. The cloak of 'national security' is routinely used to hide away from the legitimate need for public information on even the simplest national defines issues. (National security is also the excuse for the on-going brutal suppression of human rights in Kashmir valley, the North-East and the jungles of central India—the areas of age-old local rebellions—as the rest of democratic India looks away.) That some of the authoritarian features mentioned above also partially characterise a few state governments run by opposition politicians does not absolve the central government in its enhanced complicity in a massive democratic-institutional erosion.

Such erosion, to a degree, has also characterised Indonesia in recent years, even though its leader, Jokowi, is quite different from Modi, coming as he does from a background of local civil-society movements and forces of decentralisation that have been important in Indonesia since 1998. His election opponent Prabowo, an ex-general and an ex-son-in-law of Suharto, is ideologically more hostile to democracy, but in recent times Jokowi has shown some illiberal tendencies and impatience with legal procedures and law-enforcement institutions. He has tactically used corruption cases to tame political opponents and occasionally curbed freedom of association. Indonesia, unlike India, has, of course, a long legacy of suppression and violence under military and authoritarian rule.

Compared to India, Indonesia has better per capita income and poverty figures, though, as in India, job creation has been slow. Indonesia is better endowed in commodities and natural resources (of course, with the attendant predatory extraction of those natural resources by oligarchs). At times, Jokowi has attempted reducing the popular fuel subsidies and invested a great deal in infrastructure and some welfare reforms (including a substantial expansion in the coverage of the conditional cash transfer programme, PKH, and the introduction of the Village Fund grant, *Dana Desa*, which is used for purposes decided by villagers themselves). In securing universal public health care, Indonesia has been more successful than India.

Jokowi has tried to work with a coalition of disparate elements in the fragmented elite. But in recent days, with the rise of radical Islam, he has compromised with some elements of the latter who complain that he is not pious enough (despite his now-avid Friday prayers); this is most evident in his choice of vice-presidential running mate in the elections, Ma'ruf Amin, a 75-year old conservative Islamic scholar who is the Chairman of the Indonesian Ulama Council. In both India and Indonesia, the main threat to pluralist democracy is identity-based majoritarian nationalism and leaders who in furthering that cause wreck institutions that are meant to protect minority rights and preserve accountability and checks on power. In this respect, the fate of two of the largest democracies of the world remains somewhat precarious.

But, unfortunately, the corrosive effects of majoritarian ethnic nationalism may outlast any possible changes in elections or leaders. This is because they are partly rooted in deeper social changes in these transitional societies. As social and economic dislocations and uncertainties rattle such traditional societies in the development process, many individuals find solace in faith or identity-based anchors and communities. Also, in stratified societies, as some hitherto subordinate groups rise in the economic ladder, they try to legitimise their upward mobility with ostentatious adoption of cultural and religious rituals and practices that are encouraged by the sectarian political parties.

In the face of these challenges, advocates of liberal democratic institutions have to be active and imaginative in the difficult search of alternative social norms and anchors and forms of reconciling old values with new universal and inclusive human rights, beyond just forging opportunist alliances to win elections. But ultimately the survival of some minimum quality of democracy in both countries may depend less on firmly-held secular or liberal values, which are often quite shallow in the general population in spite of a long history of syncretic folk traditions, and more on the extreme social heterogeneity and divisions at all levels in both countries. The latter can, paradoxically, act as a kind of limited insurance against a long reign of intolerance or the predominance of any particular sect or creed. Social diversity can, at least up to a point, serve as a bulwark against the politics of exclusivity.

Are Indian
Democracy's Weaknesses Inherent?

Project Syndicate, 24 May 2019

Prominent in the debates around the current Indian general elections, the largest in world history, is the failure of the state in its delivery of basic public services and job-creating infrastructural facilities. These debates often use the Chinese state as an obvious comparator. There is a general impression of a purposive and effective authoritarian government in China, despite the recent excesses of Xi Jinping in consolidating his personal power. This has brought to the fore some comparative governance issues in the two countries, which are as important for liberal theory as for the practical welfare of the billions of people involved. I believe some of the key aspects here get lost in the usual simplistic authoritarianism-democracy contrasts. Authoritarianism is neither necessary nor sufficient for some of the special features of Chinese governance. Similarly, some of the dysfunctionality of Indian governance is not inherent in its democratic process.

The noteworthy feature of meritocratic recruitment and promotion (on the basis of local performance) in the Chinese bureaucracy, going back to imperial history, is absent in many other authoritarian countries. In India, even though the recruitment is on the basis of examinations, that the promotion of officials is largely on the basis of seniority and loyalty to their political masters is not essential to its democracy. The political insulation of the bureaucracy is somewhat stronger in other democracies (UK, Denmark, New Zealand), and, of course, very weak in the US (long before firing by twitter under the current President).

In meritocratic China, there is, however, plenty of evidence that at the higher echelons (at the provincial levels and beyond) promotion is largely dependent on political loyalty to particular leaders. There is quantitative evidence also of *quid pro quo* transactions in Chinese official promotions: for example, the larger the discount a provincial Party secretary gave in selling land to a firm connected with members in the national leadership, the higher in general was the chance of their promotion to the upper layer. While some of these deals have been curbed under the recent anti-corruption campaigns, there is some evidence that such campaigns are more vigorous against officials suspected to be linked with political rivals of the current leadership.

As for the organisational capacity of the state, it is usually assumed to be much higher in China than in India. There too some other considerations may prevail. First, the Indian state for all the stories about over-bureaucratisation is surprisingly small in terms of the number of public employees per capita, and unfilled vacancies in the Indian staffing of police, judiciary and bureaucracy are numerous—to a large extent these reflect the low tax revenue-raising capacity following from what for a major economy is an unusually large informal sector.

Secondly, state capacity varies between different types of state functions. The Indian state shows extraordinary capacity in some large episodic matters, like organising the complex logistics of the world's largest elections, its second largest Census and some of the world's largest religious festivals, or preparing the unique biometric identification of billion-plus people in a short period.

But the state displays poor capacity in, for example, some regular essential activities like cost effective pricing and distribution of electricity. This is not because of a lack of capable people, but more because local political considerations interfere in matters like under recovery of costs from a large and politically sensitive customer base. So a key determinant of the organisational capacity of the state is its political capacity. The police and bureaucracy are often deliberately incapacitated and made to serve short-term political goals of leaders.

Another governance issue that is not captured in the usual authoritarian-democratic distinction is that China is, and has been in history, decentralised to a surprising extent for an authoritarian country. The Party is supreme and highly centralised, but Chinese political centralisation is uniquely blended with economic and administrative decentralisation. India in some sense is the obverse—combining political decentralisation (regional power groupings have been quite strong in recent decades) with economic centralisation (the vertical fiscal imbalance, for example, with dependence of provincial governments on transfers from the central government is quite severe). Further down, in China of the total government budgetary expenditure sub-provincial levels of government tend to spend about 60%, compared to less than 10% in India. The much worse performance of sub-provincial local bodies in India in the last-mile delivery of public services and facilities is partly attributable to this. Also, acute competition among regions—induced by performance-related promotion of local officials—in business development and in carrying out experiments with new ventures has stimulated development in China more than in India (though under Xi Jinping the pace of experimentation has slowed down, along with increasing loyalty-based promotion).

All this is not to say that democracy (or its absence) does not make a difference—positive or negative—to the development process. The lack of downward accountability or electoral sanctions in China allows the leaders to avoid the pandering to short-term interests that characterises Indian politics and makes it easier for them to take bold long-term decisions relatively quickly (and independently of election-funding corporate tycoons of democracies). On the other hand, mistakes in top-level decisions or outright abuses of power (in collusion with crony business interests) take longer to detect and correct than in a situation where one regularly faces political opposition and media scrutiny. It also makes the Chinese system ultimately more brittle: in the face of a crisis the Chinese state often tends to over-react, suppress information and act heavy-handedly, thereby sometimes magnifying the dimensions of the crisis. The Indian system, for all its messiness, is more resilient. This resilience for India is in some jeopardy now as its Hindu-nationalist ruling party is using divisive and hateful tactics in polarising the electorate and weakening the institutions and processes that serve as democratic safety-valves. The outcome of the current elections will be an important signpost for India in this respect.

THE EVOLVING
POLITICAL SITUATION

Bhagwat and Bhagwati

Outlook, 19 January 2015

Recently, my old friend, Arun Shourie, was reported in the press as commenting on the new regime thus: 'You cannot talk development in Delhi and love jehad in Muzaffarnagar'. I have heard broadly similar statements from others. While I understand and appreciate the intention behind such statements, I am afraid the president of Arun's party, Amit Shah, could privately tell him: 'Yes, we can!' This, in some way, the Republican Party does every day in the US. It incites the fury of evangelicals in the Bible belt about gay marriage and abortion, while using the political capital thus garnered in pressing for tax cuts and climate change denials that warm the hearts of business-friendly people in Washington.

Nor should one indulge in the myth that 'love jihad', 'ghar wapasi' etc are the battle cries of some monkey brigade in the lunatic fringe of the Sangh Parivar. Ask Mohan Bhagwat. The economic reform-mongering cheerleaders, who want Narendra Modi to follow the sermon of the economist Bhagwati and are embarrassed by the RSS's antics, should know that Modi can try to deliver on both Bhagwat and Bhagwati.

It has been said that the Prime Minister privately expresses displeasure when the lumpen elements cross his (undefined) *Lakshmanrekha*, as reportedly happened vis-a-vis the foul-mouthed Sadhvi Jyoti. But this did not stop him from pressing her almost immediately into service in the riot-torn Trilokpuri area to mobilise Dalits against Muslims for the forthcoming elections in Delhi. Before the Lok Sabha polls, while Modi took the high ground of development and governance, he did not forget to reward a Muzaffarnagar riot-accused MP by inducting him into his cabinet. One could multiply such examples, but the general fact is that a majoritarian party can derive large electoral dividends from causing tension and polarising voters, and use the political capital to pursue business-friendly policies. This is a time-tested formula, unless it breaks out into major conflagration across large territories enough to destabilise markets. I think the Modi-RSS regime is confident that it can pursue this dual-track policy to a considerable extent, playing with small fire here and there, and containing it before it gets out of hand. Never mind the climate of suspicion and insecurity, or the large dislocations and ghettoisation of afflicted minority communities this generates.

Leave aside riots and communal tension. There is a clear division of labour in the Modi-RSS regime: Modi will look after economic governance, while the RSS agents will concentrate on education and culture. Already, RSS stooges have fanned out into influential positions in cultural and educational institutions and research funding agencies. More is forthcoming as the vacancies in them get filled. The Dinanath Batra-isation of textbooks has been going on in parts of the country for some time. At the national level, purges in the NCERT of people in charge of curriculum development have started. The cultural-nationalist project of rewriting history to reflect a mono-track 'glorious Hindu past' is in full swing. The PM himself has given leadership by publicly announcing, while inaugurating a hospital in Mumbai, that Ganesha—a case of 'grafting' an elephant's head on to a human's body— represented 'plastic surgery' in ancient India. It does not occur to the Hindu nationalist yahoos that it is a matter of national shame when the premier of a country does this. Ernest Renan, a 19th century French historian, is reported to have said that nationalism in a country is 'about getting its history wrong'; but even he probably could not imagine such outrageous blurring of history and mythology that feeds into Hindu cultural nationalism.

Of course the damage in India is so pervasive because the tentacles of the state are deeply implicated in the control of educational and cultural institutions. The Congress and the Left in the past have merrily indulged in this, without bothering to create the necessary institutional insulation and autonomy against the ravages of political patronage and opportunism. The only difference with the earlier regime is that the number of bigots, charlatans and mediocrities is much larger in the RSS brigade. The continuing institutional decay is thus likely to be accelerated.

Meanwhile, on the economic development front, while the current government is undoubtedly more energetic, not much has yet happened beyond empty rhetoric and exhortations and some tinkering with bureaucratic procedures. The 'Make in India' slogan is collecting a 'like' every 3 seconds on Facebook, but there is not much evidence that important players have taken it seriously. There is a need for investment in public infrastructure, the key constraint in the Indian economy, but given the fiscal deficit, the corporate debt hangover, the staggering burden of accumulated bad loans in the books of public banks and the corresponding need for massive recapitalisation, and the impasse in the restructuring of the whole design and implementation of public-private partnerships, it is difficult to envisage substantial changes in Indian manufacturing anytime soon. The promises of jobs and 'achhe din' with which Modi's oratory had fired up India's youth at election time will, therefore, take much too long to materialise.

In the social sector, the Swachh Bharat Abhiyan, started with great fanfare and broom-wielding photo-ops, cannot make a big dent at the problem of sanitation, certainly not without an adequate understanding of why many toilets created under the Nirmal Bharat Abhiyan of the earlier government remain unused to this day. In healthcare, the universal health plan expected to be launched by the PM this April (2015) under the National Health Assurance Mission is estimated to cost 1.6 trillion rupees over four years, and yet there have been news reports of a near 20 per cent cut in the Union health ministry budget next year in a country with already one of the lowest health spending to GDP ratio.

In general, the contradictions in the government's slogans and implementation are rather breathtaking. We know about 'minimum government, maximum governance'—how this is achieved by a government that works through a vast unreformed bureaucracy answerable mainly to the PMO and a large cabinet of political lightweights and subordinates, who, with few exceptions, are not well-known for their competence, is anybody's guess. Modi says he does not believe in 'reform by stealth', and yet many of the important changes so far in implementation of laws are being pursued quietly through administrative 'notifications' (changes in environment clearances and forest rights, with a suspension of earlier mandatory consultations and hearings with local people), ordinances (whittling down consent requirements and social impact assessment in the Land Acquisition Act), procedural changes and cuts in budget allocations in NREGA (supposed to 'guarantee' work on demand), and so on. The PM never tires of proclaiming his faith in 'cooperative federalism', yet he has centralised much of the governing authority in the country in his PMO; in his newest creation of Niti Aayog, while the details are not fully clear, the financial allocations for centrally sponsored programmes appear now to have been transferred to the ministry of finance, presumably bypassing any serious consultation on the allocations with the state governments in the National Development Council or Inter-State Council. In a recent speech, Modi said criticism was necessary in a healthy democracy, and yet is afraid to meet critical questions from the media (instead, he prefers sending out Twitter messages and has in the past walked out of a live TV programme where he was uncomfortable with the questions); all his ministers have been strictly instructed to avoid the media (some have responded to questions by the media with a common refrain: 'woh batayenge'). All this when a large part of the media is still quite fawning.

The Prime Minister prostrates himself before the Parliament on his first day and lauds India's democracy as 'the best gift our constitution-makers have given us', yet is silent when the democratic rights of individuals are regularly trampled upon by thugs in RSS-affiliated or like-minded organisations when they find fault with a particular book, artwork or film.

Narendra Modi is the leader of a party that has now appropriated Gandhi (while openly violating his views on tolerance, minorities, conversion and other issues), and at the same time worships Savarkar (and possibly at the proposed Nathuram Godse temple when it comes up in Meerut).

Yes, the Modi-RSS regime can thrive in this welter of contradictions. The head of development and governance can be grafted on to the body of Hindu fanaticism, and like Ganesha, can be a marvel of our ancient plastic surgery skills.

The Deep Crisis in Higher Education in India—What to Do?

Indian Express, 20 January 2017

Let me start with a blunt statement: India's higher education is in general a decrepit, dilapidated system, it's afflicted by a deep malaise.

The National Knowledge Commission—Report to the Nation (2006-09) put it only a bit more mildly: 'There is a quiet crisis in higher education in India which runs deep'. Three widely acknowledged criteria for judging an education system: Access, Equity, and Quality. We have failed our young people by all three criteria.

On account of financial hardship, inferior schools, lack of remedial education and social compulsions for early marriage for girls, the majority of young people from poor families drop out of school at or before completing secondary education. So they have no access to higher education. In addition, for socially disadvantaged groups discrimination at workplace and occupational segregation lower the rate of return from (and hence demand for) higher education for them compared to other groups.

Even for those who complete secondary education and are willing to enter, entry into premier higher education institutions is riddled with various kinds of inequity (only marginally relieved for some people by lower-caste reservations). For example, the currently almost indispensable intensive entry examination preparation in coaching classes (or private tuition) with high fees is often out of reach for poor students. (NSS data suggest that in 2014 nearly 60% of male students in the 18-24 age group cite financial constraints or engagement in economic activities as the reason for discontinuing higher education.)

The quality of most higher education institutions in India is abysmal. Let me elaborate on this.

In terms of quantity, the expansion of higher education has been impressive. At the time of Independence, we had about 20 universities and fewer than 500 colleges in the whole country. In 2014-15, there were 760 universities and more than 38,000 colleges, catering to about 34 million students. But the expansion in quantity has often been at the expense of quality.

There is extreme faculty shortage, apart from stark deficiencies in the matters of library books, laboratory facilities, computer and broadband internet, classrooms and buildings, etc. As much as 30 to 50% of faculty positions are vacant in many institutions. Many faculty posts are filled by under-qualified 'temporary' recruits.

Two-thirds of enrolment in higher education are in private institutions (the majority of them, according to NSS data, say that there were not enough government institutions nearby or where they could get admission). Fees at private institutions are more than double those charged at government institutions. In parts of western and southern India with a large expansion of for-profit private colleges with high 'capitation fees' and politically managed loans from public banks, politicians have entered into the business of higher education in a big way, turning colleges into lucrative degree-giving factories.

There are many familiar accounts of rote-learning, outdated curriculum, and just cramming for exams. There are severe learning deficits in our institutions of higher education. Just to give one example: in a recent survey of MA 2nd year students in Economics in a reputed state university in Maharashtra, reported in the *Economic and Political Weekly*, students were asked 6 simple questions from the basic class VI school textbook in Mathematics; only 11 out of 200 students could answer all of them correctly.

The (erstwhile) Planning Commission had estimated that only 17.5% of our graduates are employable. Many of the graduates lack even basic language and cognitive skills. In the Information Technology sector, NASSCOM, the main chamber of commerce, estimates that even for engineering graduates, only 20% of graduates of engineering colleges in India are employable in IT companies.

In terms of quality of post-graduate research, while some of it is no doubt significant, over all our research quality is much below the world average. It has been widely noted that India does not have a single university in the top 200 in the world rankings (China has about 10 universities in that list).

The international rankings are far from perfect, but many of the Indian complaints against them sound like 'sour grapes'. There is no doubt that India lags behind (compared to even some developing countries) in most metrics, particularly in terms of population or GDP—full-time researchers, papers published, scholarly citation impact, number of patents taken out, and so on.

So if most of our graduates learn very little and are not employable, and the very poor drop out anyway, and there is meagre world-class research going on, what is the point of this higher education system?

Reformers, like many in the past, have tried to tweak the system here and there, with very little effect. One has to think in terms of a quantum leap.

I know in today's circumstances thinking of a complete overhaul over the next 20 years or so may be recklessly utopian, but not completely useless if we want to think big and draw up a plan for fundamental changes. I am obviously skipping the formidable (though not insuperable) problems of transition and for now mainly concentrating on the major goals. Below is my suggested plan in broad contours. On account of constraints of time and space, I am leaving out many of the nuances and qualifications which should be part of a fuller treatment. The financial requirements of the whole plan also need to be worked out.

In my plan all school-leaving students should have universal access at near-zero tuition fees with option to join two alternative streams:

One towards local vocational institutes to learn different skills (like plumbing, welding, carpentry, auto mechanics, driving, nursing, policing, firefighting, and so on)

These institutes should be spread out all over a state, with facilities also for evening classes.

After 2 years, students with enough class credits and after passing a test will earn a diploma.

Funding of these institutes should be shared between the state and the business community (with a special cess on medium to large business)—the latter will benefit for having the chance (and incentive) to monitor and directly employ (or get as apprentice) some of the graduating students, with recruitment offices in the institute itself. (This draws somewhat on the current German model.)

The other alternative stream will go to a 3-year local college where general science and humanities subjects will be taught. The main purpose will be to train school teachers, clerks, accountants, actuaries, lab and library assistants, basic programmers, and so on. After 3 years students with enough class credits and after passing a test will earn a degree.

The funding will be borne entirely by the state. (This is somewhat like the California Community College model.)

The top 10% of streams (a) and (b), if they pass appropriate entry tests, will be allowed to enter two alternative streams at a higher level (d) or (e):

Professional schools (in subjects like Law, Business, Engineering and Medical). Here the tuition fees will be high, but with availability of a large number of student loans, repayable in the first five years of the student's getting a job. Some of these schools can be private, others state-funded.

Public universities, of which there should not be more than 50 in the whole country. The subjects taught will be specialised branches of science and humanities. Again, the fees will be high, but with availability of a large number of student loans, repayable in the first five years of the student's getting a job. The financial and faculty resources that are currently spread thin in more than 700 universities should be conserved and more effectively used in not more than 50 universities (roughly 2 for each major state).

The top 1% of streams (d) and (e), if they pass appropriate entry tests, will be allowed to enter a World-class Research University, of which there should be not more than two in the whole country. Tuition will be free and everybody will have a scholarship. The funding will be entirely by the state. For the sake of stimulating in India the current world-wide trend in collaborative research across disciplines, departments should be reorganised with a focus on multi-disciplinary research.

With this structure in mind, I shall now have some remarks on the functioning and administration, faculty recruitment and promotion, etc in these higher education institutions, particularly in streams (d), (e), and (f).

No involvement by politicians, administrators or regulators (like UGC) in personnel selection, particularly in any of those three streams, neither in the selection of officials like a college principal or VC, nor in the appointment or promotion of faculty, nor in the conduct of the examination system. This is, of course, most difficult to achieve in India, and quite contrary to the persistent government initiatives (including the new Education Bill with the Lok Sabha). Every education minister, either at the state or central level, believes that as the government provides the money, he or she (and the associated bureaucrats) have the right to interfere in the running of the college or the university. This is a curse of the Indian higher education system that must be exorcised. Every three years or so a public college or university should, after an independent audit, be accountable to the legislature on explaining how the total budget assigned has been spent, but the latter should have no say on personnel selection or internal governance matters. The best public universities in the world are mainly free of outside involvement.

Faculty selection and promotion should be entirely the responsibility of the faculty in consultation with outside (both outside the department and outside the university) faculty members in peer review. In (a) and (b) institutions, the main criterion for judging faculty will be teaching quality (partly depending on serious and anonymous student evaluations for each course). In (d), (e), and (f) institutions, of course, along with teaching, quality of research will be evaluated by peers inside and outside departments and impact of publications, including in recognised international outlets. In new appointments, instead of interviews by closed-door selection committees, the candidates on a short list should be invited to present a research paper in an open seminar, where the candidates should be answerable to questions and criticisms by anyone present. After appointment, every three years each faculty member, junior or senior, should have a merit review by a departmental and university committee (with some outside referees). No seniority-based promotion is to be allowed.

With a positive merit review, salaries should be adjusted upwards. The salary structure should be sufficiently flexible, within some well-defined general parameters, so that exceptional merit judged by peer review can be rewarded. The current system of academic salary structure linked to civil service rules and scales, periodically revised by the Pay Commission, should be discarded.

The new technology of distance learning should be fully utilised in upgrading the teaching and knowledge standards. Particularly in streams (b), (d) and (e), we should take advantage of the basic courses currently being offered in the international Massive Open Online Courses (MOOCs) system, expanding on a big scale the current Indianised version being tried out in some of the IITs and IIMs. These courses should be aligned with associated topic-wise tutorials by the current faculty. Apart from quality upgrading, this can also partly relieve our acute shortage of qualified faculty. Of course, the constraints of inadequate facility of students in English medium of international teaching and dearth of internet access will continue to limit this for quite some time.

Our higher academic institutions remain in splendid Brahminical isolation from the surrounding economy and society in their locations, though, alas, not from the local sectarian and party politics. In the US, the connection between the ongoing research in universities and the innovations in the local industrial and commercial economy is quite impressive. The Indian experience is often dismal in this respect.

Just to give an example from a locality nearby: I have heard stories that Howrah, which used to be a major centre of light engineering products, declined over time throwing off thousands of jobs, partly because it failed to carry out some simple technical innovations (which its competitors around the world managed). Yet, in Howrah there was a thriving engineering college nearby (BE college, now a university), which was a potential source of collaboration in these innovations, but there was no established forum or mechanism for any connection or interaction.

Similarly in social sciences, there is ample scope for our Economics and Sociology students to carry out their honours and post-graduate research projects using field survey data from the local bazaars and neighbourhoods (including slums where our maid servants and cobblers live).

Let me now discuss an important downside to the principle of non-interference by administrators and politicians that I have advocated. With full autonomy, some colleges and universities can degenerate into cosy, nepotistic clubs of rampant mediocrity. Sociologist Diego Gambetta has described such a system of collusive mediocrity in Italian universities, which will not be unfamiliar in some Indian universities—a culture of mediocrity where mediocre people get other mediocre people around them and thrive in a cocoon of comfortable cronyism. Autonomy vs cronyism is the inexorable dilemma of a higher education system.

In the US, this problem has been mostly averted by a culture of constant competition among the better universities— they raid one another for the best faculty, and try to generate a critical mass of good faculty and students. Students also gravitate to where the best faculty are. When professors move from one university to another, they move with the whole paraphernalia of funded research projects, labs and affiliated students. So it'll be costly for a university to lose its good faculty members, if it fails to provide a stimulating environment.

It is, of course, not easy to reproduce this culture of competition and mobility everywhere, but one can try, with some external monitoring mechanisms in place.

Periodic reviews of a whole department by outside professional peer groups (of academics, not bureaucrats), particularly if the review report is taken seriously by the external financial authorities in the allocation of faculty slots to the department, can be a significant deterrent to indulgence in mediocrity. In many fields, research grants from external funding agencies are an important source of finance for a US university (in the form of overhead costs charged to the grant), and mediocre people failing to get such grants can become financially costly for a university. For this to work, the Indian research funding agencies (like UGC, ICSSR, ICHR, CSIR, etc) themselves need to be shorn of the current overload of bureaucratic control.

Apart from mediocre faculty, the other problem of autonomy may be in encouraging low-quality degree giving. The solution to this is not state or regulatory interference (we are familiar, for example, with many scandals in the examination system under such interference). The ultimate solution will have to be the market test. Job-givers will not value such degrees given by colleges or universities that abuse their autonomy, and students will soon find this out.

Finally, a word or two on the acute and potentially overwhelming political and sociological issues. The vested interests in the current stagnation are quite powerful—politicians, bureaucrats, mediocre faculty, etc.

As Machiavelli had observed five centuries back:

The reformer has enemies in all those who profit by the old order, and only lukewarm defenders in all those who would profit by the new.

Nothing will happen unless the potential beneficiaries of change get organised. It is easy to run down any substantial proposal to improve quality as elitist. When it comes to academic excellence, I am unashamedly an elitist. Even in Communist countries, say in the erstwhile Soviet Union (or China today), the Academy of the various Sciences, for example, were (are) highly elitist. What is important to me is ensuring equality of opportunity to everybody. But that does not mean equality of outcome.

In India, the default redistributive option for politicians has been caste reservations in admissions to higher education institutions for the disadvantaged. But when these institutions keep on churning out graduates who are mostly unemployable, I believe the consciousness will rise among our poor and middle classes and castes that the way forward is to fight the vested interests and move in the direction of improving education quality, along with access and equity.

At the same time, we have to understand that equity is not ensured simply by ensuring free and universal access, as we have proposed for our streams (a) and (b). It is also not just a matter of arranging for enough scholarships and remedial courses for students from disadvantaged backgrounds, many of whom are first-generation entrants to the higher education system. In the social churning that India is going through many of our colleges and universities have become sites of contestation for our larger social conflicts. Given this context, we have to nurture an enabling and empowering atmosphere and institutional culture for these new entrants in an alien environment of long domination by upper classes and castes. Rohith Vemula's tragic suicide and last letter at the Central University of Hyderabad (in 2016) point to the many challenges we face in our long road to equity in the field of education. But equity and quality need not work at cross purposes, and it is our duty to convince the political leaders of all groups about the importance and feasibility of these two goals working together.

The Grand Hoaxes

Indian Express, 5 August 2017

As the triumphal march of the Modi-Shah juggernaut continues, smashing the feckless and disorganised Opposition on its way, it is useful to ponder over at least two of the grand hoaxes of the current regime over the last three years that have been impressively successful with the general electorate.

The first one, endlessly repeated in the election campaigns of 2014, was the promise of moving away from the politics of 'dole' of the UPA regime, towards that of massive job creation, reproducing the dazzlingly successful 'Gujarat model of development' in the rest of India. This appealed to the 'aspirational' youth, particularly in North India, where there has been a youth bulge in the demographics. That the Gujarat model of high growth was not really an exemplar in job creation (a substantial part of Gujarat manufacturing growth was in highly capital-intensive activities like petroleum refineries and petro-chemicals) did not deter that appeal.

In the last three years, it is now clear to even the fawning media and politicians that the pace of job creation has not been particularly shining. Some data (for example those of the Labour Bureau for a select number of mainly labour-intensive industries) show even a job decline. In particular, regular formal sector jobs, which is what the aspirational youth hanker after as they leave the low-productivity jobs in agriculture, have remained a tiny proportion of the total employment. The backlog of 'surplus workers' (as estimated in the India Employment Report 2016 on the basis of National Sample Survey data) exceeds 50 million workers. As the glittering job promises by the 'vikas purush' fade, inevitably the diversionary tactics on the way to 2019 increasingly involve the polarising, majoritarian, poison-fuming 'Hindutva' machinery of the ruling party going into overdrive.

If the supreme leader cannot give you good jobs, he can at least impress you with his valiant fight against the demon of corruption. Even if you dismiss the election promise of getting Rs 15 lakh in everybody's bank account from the foreign-stashed corrupt money as what BJP president Amit Shah called 'jumla', you cannot ignore the bold launching of the 'brahmastra' of demonetisation in November 2016. This has turned out to be one of the grandest hoaxes in Indian political history.

First, the objective was to vaporise the corrupt cash hoarded by the rich, then to eliminate counterfeit money, then the source of terrorists' finance, and finally to stimulate the use of digital money. Now as the Reserve Bank keeps on counting the returned notes for eternity, it is clear to everybody that either the hoarded cash was puny or was deftly returned with impunity by the hoarders.

(Some people even suspect that maybe the Reserve Bank does not want to admit that they have got back more notes than they had circulated, possibly because demonetisation has provided an opportunity to legalise even some of the counterfeit money.) As for encouraging the use of digital money, many other countries have done that without anywhere near the enormous hardship of demonetisation.

We now have plenty of evidence of the hardship, and not just from the bank queues that the urban middle classes experienced. Primary survey data from wholesale and retail traders around Bengaluru suggest an average fall of 20 per cent in sales in December-January (about one-fifth of the respondents reporting more than a 40 per cent drop in sales). A survey in December-January (*Economic & Political Weekly,* 6 May 2017) 2016-17 showed that in Panipat, a textile hub of North India, there was a collapse of domestic business sales of 40 per cent to 80 per cent—as a result, about half of 3,50,000 workers employed there were laid off, and there was no cash to pay wages.

The Prime Minister cited GDP data to taunt 'Harvard' academics; his economic advisers did not dare tell him that those short-term GDP calculations, based mainly on projections from formal sector data, are meaningless in capturing the real GDP changes in the vast informal sector in times of economic shocks like demonetisation.

Yet, and this is the political magic of the hoax, people thought—and we have survey evidence to back it—that all this hardship was worth bearing for the greater cause of fighting corruption and punishing the dishonest rich, even as the latter actually got off quite well.

In general, the PR campaign has succeeded in creating the impression—and the media have gone along with it—that the current regime is much cleaner. Let us ignore the gigantic Vyapam scam or the Lalit Modi scandal in BJP-run states. The auctions for natural resources are now much cleaner, people say. Actually they started being cleaner, under Supreme Court orders, in the last years of the UPA regime.

Also, with the international mining boom over, there is now less money to be made in these sectors. No action has been reported to be taken on the findings of the Directorate of Revenue Intelligence (DRI) on the cases of large over-invoicing of power equipment and coal imports by some of the big corporate houses. Many stories about continuing corruption in government procurement and land grabs continue, but the DRI and Enforcement Directorate (ED) are not overly active in pursuing them if they involve ruling party politicians, and the intimidated NGOs and media largely keep quiet.

Then there is the elephant in the room, the matter of large election funding, particularly for the ruling party. Political parties have been exempt from RTI and retrospectively from FCRA (a blunt instrument regularly used to harass NGOs). The attempts at so-called reform in the form of 'election bonds' have made matters even less transparent.

Meanwhile, the Whistle-blowers Act is being diluted, and the authority for tax raids given even to junior officers has multiplied opportunities for extortion. But people believe—and the hired trolls will go on screaming—that the spectacular slaying of the demon of corruption is continuing and that's what counts in our leaders' triumphal march towards an Opposition-mukt majoritarian semi-authoritarianism.

Diffusing the Jobs Time Bomb

Times of India, 30 October 2017

Many people think that one of the major economic failures of the current government is in the area of jobs. It came to power promising jobs for 'aspirational India' in place of 'doles'. While 'doles' remain largely in place, Labour Bureau data seem to suggest even an absolute decline in formal sector jobs over the last three years, instead of any significant rise.

The backlog of 'surplus workers' that include the underemployed in all sectors (as estimated in the India Employment Report 2016) exceeds 50 million workers—this does not include the women who are often discouraged dropouts from the labour force. Rhetoric or electoral 'jumla' aside jobs, particularly formal sector regular jobs which the young in India hanker after, have been a chronic problem over several decades.

If one takes the whole period since 1972-73 when National Sample Survey started collecting employment and unemployment data on a comprehensive basis, job growth has been relatively sluggish (except for short spells, as in the first decade of this century, and that too mainly in the construction sector). Many alternative solutions for the job problem have been suggested, like larger investment in infrastructure (particularly electricity and roads), education and credit to small and medium enterprises. Some of these involve structural problems which can be resolved only in the medium to long run.

Others have pointed to stringent labour laws which inhibit firing (and therefore hiring) labour. Some state governments have relaxed those stringent laws over the last three years and it may be too early yet to find much conclusive evidence of that making a big difference in job creation. My own empirical hunch has been that labour law is a constraint, but it may not be the most important or even a binding constraint.

While the job crisis remains severe and potentially explosive in the socio-political sphere, three possible ways of relieving it have not received adequate attention.

First, a policy of wage or payroll subsidies. A significant part of current budgetary subsidies, both at the central and state levels, are in the form of capital subsidies—subsidies on interest or credit and tax concessions of various kinds for capital investment. We do not have precise estimates, but my back-of-the-envelope calculations suggest that these subsidies may come to 5% of GDP. A part of these subsidies, which currently encourage capital intensive methods of production, may be converted into wage subsidies.

In fact, the same businessman in the formal sector may be paid the subsidies, but now for hiring more people rather than machines. A cap may be imposed on the wage subsidy on any particular job so that the incentive remains on hiring more people than on paying large salaries to particular employees. Similarly, possible scams in the form of fake payrolls may be avoided with appropriate biometric identification.

A second suggestion relates to skill formation. The current Skill India programme has not made much progress. The ministry of skill development has now abandoned the earlier much-hyped but unattainable target of training at least 300 million workers in new skills by 2022. Currently, less than 5% of the total work force has formal vocational skills. Of about 3 million people who have received some training by July 2017 under the current scheme, less than 10% have reportedly received any job offers.

One possible remedy may be to encourage the business sector (particularly in local clusters) to get involved in the training of workers somewhat in the line of the German model, the world's most successful vocational training programme. German business largely funds such programmes as this gives them an opportunity to look for and get as apprentice good-quality workers. In any case, a vocational programme that is not integrated with a job placement programme is unlikely to be viable.

A third suggestion relates to the agricultural sector. While most young people even in farmer families now want to get out of their traditional occupation, whether one likes it or not, the demographics and occupational distribution of our labour force is such that for a long time agriculture will have to continue to be a main source of jobs. The important task is to make those jobs more productive and higher-paying.

The area where India has a large potential is in non-crop agriculture—fruits, vegetables and livestock farming. These activities are also highly labour intensive. But for making this sector more productive and job creating at least two essential pre-requisites are

    (a) investment in cold chains and refrigerated transport; and

    (b) streamlining the marketing arrangements.

Agricultural marketing remains one of the most unreformed and cartelised sectors in India. More direct farm-to-shop arrangements with minimum involvement of collusive intermediaries have to be forged. Our farms are (and will remain for quite some time) too small. They have to be amalgamated into farming companies or cooperatives at least for the sake of marketing (and input provision). The Amul model of collecting from small producers and then cooperatively marketing and distributing has to be extended all over India in these productive sectors of non-crop agriculture if profitable job creation is our objective.

These suggestions for job growth are within the realm of feasibility even in the short to intermediate time horizon. Meanwhile, the time bomb of not enough jobs for our young people keeps ticking.

'Anti-National' Thoughts

Indian Express, 10 April 2019

Whichever party wins the parliamentary election of 2019, the real long-term challenge is to stem the rot of institutional foundations.

The headlines say that the ruling party manifesto emphasises nationalism ('nation first'), and, on the economic front, it will aspire to make India the third-largest economy in the world by the end of the next decade, to make it reach the list of top 50 countries in the ranking of Ease of Doing Business, and repeats the old promise of doubling farmers' income by 2022.

In the West, there is an old saying that 'patriotism is the last refuge of the scoundrel'. But what do foreigners know about the glories of Hindu nationalism? Gandhiji regarded armed nationalism a 'curse'. Tagore wrote in 1908:

> Patriotism cannot be our final spiritual shelter; my refuge is humanity. I'll not buy glass for the price of diamonds, and I'll never allow patriotism to triumph as long as I live.

But both Gandhiji and Tagore are long dead.

On the economic front, while most economists believe that, whichever party is in power, unless there is some disaster,

India will be the third-largest economy in the world by the end of the next decade, there is hardly any respectable economist who believes that as things have been going, farmers' income can be doubled by 2022—it's just a 'jumla'.

The current government puts a lot of value on India's place in the World Bank's ranking on Ease of Doing Business, and took a victory lap when it improved significantly in recent years. (It is not particularly hard to 'game' the system, as we know that it is based on data collected from only two cities, Mumbai and Delhi. The Chinese are even better than us in gaming it, they had an even larger increase in the ranks in the same years.) Nevertheless, an improvement in those ranks is a good sign.

But around the same time, when the World Bank came out with the Ease of Doing Business rankings, another part of the same Bank came out with rankings of Human Capital Index, evaluating performance on health and education. In this, India not only has a very low rank, it is even lower than that of two of our poorer neighbours, Nepal and Bangladesh. When these rankings hit the press, one central minister in Delhi told a journalist, 'we do not accept the data'. Of course, we accept data only when they go in our favour! There have been more recent examples of this. On the social front, recently Amnesty International came out with the data that Uttar Pradesh now tops in the number of hate crimes in India, but then who does not know that Amnesty International is an infamous agency whose main goal is to malign us!

Unfortunately, international organisations keep churning out data of a similar kind: In the Social Hostilities Index, brought out by the Pew Research Center for 198 countries, at the end of 2016 India was among the eight worst countries. In the World Press Freedom Index, brought out by Reporters without Borders, in 2017-18 India's rank among 180 countries was low, at 138. In the Rule of Law Index brought out by the World Justice Project for 113 countries, in 2017-18 India's rank was 62. In the Report of the Economist Intelligence Unit on the State of Democracy in the World for 2018, India is in the category of 'flawed', not full, democracy; out of 167 countries, India's rank is 41, worse than Latvia, Taiwan or Botswana—the rank for India having sharply declined compared to 2014.

The current government has no doubt had some laudable economic achievements in providing some measure of financial inclusion, roads, housing, sanitation, gas for cooking fuel, etc. for the poor, and streamlining GST (though clumsily implemented) and insolvency procedures for business. But actual progress in much of these has not matched the constant barrage of official hype, and the Indian economy, particularly in the vast informal sector, has barely recovered from the whimsical onslaught of demonetisation in November 2016 thought up by an ignorant but arrogant leadership and carried out by a confused and unprepared banking bureaucracy.

The general expectation, however, is that supercharged jingoism will see the ruling party through. Whichever party wins the election, the real long-term challenge is to stem the rot of institutional foundations. The institutional decay hollowing out the shell of democracy started a few decades back, but it has accelerated. The executive overreach and abuse have dissipated the independence of police and bureaucracy, with tax and investigative agencies blithely used for personal vendetta of leaders and for cynical stirring, or keeping on slow boil, of the anti-corruption investigations for continual smearing of Opposition politicians, while cases against the ruling party politicians (or any new allies who are lured to their fold) are quietly dropped.

Attempts to enfeeble the independence of regulatory bodies are common—even apex bodies like the Reserve Bank of India, the Supreme Court or the Election Commission of India have come under pressure. The centralisation of all power in the PMO, apart from making a mockery of the oft-repeated rhetoric of 'cooperative federalism', has rendered the cabinet system of government largely ineffective. The legislature is used mainly for acclamation and hurried passing, without much discussion, of complex bills. The joint parliamentary committees that raise questions are starved of information and/or ignored.

Dissent is often branded as sedition and as 'anti-national'—even though it is arguable that judged by the frequent violations of the Constitution in letter and spirit and of the civic nationalism that is based on constitutional values it is the ruling party and its affiliate organisations that are in some sense deeply anti-national. The Prime Minister, who is quite effusive on all manner of things in his one-way tweets and radio chats, falls eerily silent when inconvenient truths or atrocities by his party affiliates hit the news. While never hesitating in stressing his own muscular brand of leadership, he is strangely afraid to meet the press or any searching questions from journalists and legislators. He is open only to the part of the media that is fawning and to adulatory crowds. The cloak of 'national security' is routinely used to hide away from the legitimate need for public information on even the simplest national defence issues.

National security is also the excuse for the ongoing suppression of human rights in Kashmir valley, the North-East and the jungles of central India—the areas of age-old local rebellions—as the rest of democratic India looks away. But then it is 'anti-national' to even mention these things.

From False Hopes to False Pride

Indian Express, 15 June 2019

Narendra Modi's stunning victory in the recent general elections of 2019 is no doubt a great personal achievement for a leader whose oratorical and political skills (often tinged with a bit of venom) are indeed impressive and matched by indefatigable energy. Of course, he has been helped by disproportionately large corporate donations that gave him a megaphone to drown other voices, by a largely supine media that, apart from allowing him to escape hard questioning, became used to blowing his trumpet, by a fragmentary Opposition with immature leadership, by an army of volunteers canvassing both door-to-door and via WhatsApp, and, of course, a last-stage unexpected gift from Masood Azhar in the form of a terrorist incident to 'boldly' respond to. But all this is not enough to fully explain the victory that Indian voters have handed him.

These are early days to carry out a full analysis of the electoral data for deciphering the range of explanatory factors, but there are enough straws in the wind to venture some guesses. First, it is unlikely that the economic achievements of the Modi regime played much of a role, and it is not a coincidence that the ruling party campaigns, particularly in periods of apparent desperation, did not much emphasise them either. Some did talk about toilets (though the actual use of those toilets lagged far behind their bureaucratic targets of construction) and gas cylinders for the poor (though evidence suggests refills of those cylinders lagged far behind their initial acquisition), but their impact on voting behaviour was likely to have been marginal (as suggested by the opinion polls by mid-February). One, of course, did not hear much about the slaying of the dragon of corruption through demonetisation, the grand hoax of November 2016. The stories of agrarian distress, which led to the hurried start of the PM-KISAN scheme, did not melt away and with the current state of land records, the two-hectare limit in the scheme must have been a block in implementation in large parts of the country. The other economic concern about the lack of good jobs for young people remained uppermost in many a mind, a promise of 2014 obviously belied.

People often talked about Modi's incorruptibility, but the same was true of Manmohan Singh, the leader of a regime associated with corruption scandals. Corruption is not necessarily associated with dynastic politics. Even if it were, the latter is not completely absent in the ruling party (a significant fraction of its MPs are 'dynasts'), and its NDA partners. More importantly, there is only a thin line between public corruption and crony capitalism which has been rampant in both UPA and NDA regimes. Besides, in India's system of highly secretive election funding—made murkier by electoral bonds—a party far ahead of others in benefiting from that system cannot deny complicity.

There have been many accounts of young people telling press reporters that they may not have jobs, but Modi has ensured that India is respected in the league of nations. Undoubtedly, this has been important to many voters. This kind of preening nationalism is based on a deep inferiority complex, that the rest of the world does not give us enough respect. Many people abroad have not been much impressed by India's actions in the Balakot airstrike, and, many in India are unaware that India's reputation abroad has substantially declined as well in several respects under the Modi regime. India used to be respected for its pluralism and democracy. In the widely-cited report of the Economist Intelligence Unit on the State of Democracy in the World for 2018, India's rank declined sharply in just four years since 2014. The lynchings of Muslims, atrocities on Dalits, the assault on some universities by goons and politicians, the repression of dissent, and the prominence given by the regime to Hindu supremacists (like Yogi Adityanath or Pragya Thakur) have brought us disgrace in the civilised world. Politicians pontificating on plastic surgery or test-tube babies by ancient Hindus, or rants against evolution or the cancer-curing properties of cow urine, have made us a laughing stock in the world. Yet, in our echo-chambers, there will be non-stop hype about the Modi regime raising our national prestige.

Yes, nationalism can have a positive role in unifying people and transcending internecine group conflicts, but the kind of ethnic pseudo-nationalism that the RSS/BJP propagates is highly divisive, not unifying. If it is really the case that, as some people believe, Modi's appeal can cut across castes and regions, and therefore, is a positive step for India, then this nationalism has to transcend majoritarian ethnicity. It has to be, instead, a kind of 'constitutional nationalism, based on our constitutional values and norms. Modi once called the Constitution his 'holy book', but that has been mere empty rhetoric; in reality, he has connived with his party members and associates, frequently violating the Constitution in letter and spirit. Majoritarianism is not democracy—I don't like the oxymoronic term 'illiberal democracy', used by many people, from Fareed Zakaria to Viktor Orban, as this ignores in some sense the essence of democracy. Effectively turning nearly 200 million people in our country into intimidated, second-class citizens is a violation of that constitutional nationalism, however, impressive Modi's electoral victory may be. Concentration of power in one person, intimidation of critics and dissenters, weakening of institutions of checks and balances and misuse of police, bureaucracy, tax and investigative agencies against political opponents, are all gross violations of the Constitution which can put the world's largest democracy to shame.

If the victory in 2014 was partly based on false hope, then that of 2019 seems based on false pride.

The Pluralistic Idea
of India being Dismantled

Indian Express, 12 October 2019

In the world's largest half-democracy, we have by now got used to a constant barrage of spin, half-truths and lies which has successfully hijacked the legacy of past leaders for its own cause—Gandhiji, Patel, Netaji Bose, Bhagat Singh, Vivekananda and even Ambedkar—although all of them were openly against the idea of 'Hindutva', as currently interpreted, and Hindu Rashtra. In the sphere of ideology, the idea of nationalism is in the process of being hijacked. Already for many in our country (including the hysterically cheer-leading sections of the media), nationalism is narrowly taken as majoritarianism in the service of a jingoistic state and focused on hating a neighbouring country (and, of course, 'enemies within'). The British politician, Nye Bevan, after his first visit to Pakistan in its early days is reported to have thus described that country: 'I have never been to a country so much in love with hate'. Unfortunately, we are fast reaching a situation where this description may fit our country as well.

Religion-based nationalism as propagated by Jinnah, and opposed by Gandhiji, was the basis of the formation of Pakistan. All over the world today, ethnic nationalism of one kind or another is making a comeback—Christian nationalism in Poland and Hungary, white nationalism among evangelical Christians in the US, Slavic and orthodox-church based nationalism in Russia, Islamic nationalism in Turkey and Indonesia and so on. About a hundred years back, the leaders of social thinking in India applied their mind to what should be the basis of nationalism in the diverse, extremely heterogeneous society of India. I have particularly in mind the thoughts of Gandhiji and Tagore on nationalism expressed in various forms (essays and lectures by both, and in the case of Tagore, also in literature with several poems and at least three novels—one of which later was the basis of a widely-known Satyajit Ray movie, *Ghare Baire*) in the first three decades of the 20th century.

They were, of course, both anti-imperialists, thus sharing in the popular movements of nationalism against colonial rulers, but they wanted to go beyond this to think about a more positive basis of nationalism. Both of them found the nation-state of European history, with a singular social homogenising principle and militarised borders and jingoistic mobilisation against supposed enemy states, unacceptable and unsuitable for India's diverse society. Instead, they both drew upon the long folk-syncretic tradition of Indian society (which grew out of the layers of sediments formed by successive waves of social reform and rebellion, called the bhakti movements, against the dominance of the rigid Hindu brahminical system, over many centuries in different parts of India), extolling inter-faith tolerance and pluralism, and wanted to make that the constructive basis of Indian nationalism.

Both Gandhiji and Tagore were deeply religious persons. But Gandhiji openly said, 'Free India will not be a Hindu Raj; it will be an Indian Raj, based not on the majority of any religious sect or community'. Tagore was trenchant in his criticism of the western idea of the nation-state, 'with all its paraphernalia of power and prosperity, its flags and pious hymns . . . its mock thunders of patriotic bragging', and of how it stokes a national conceit that makes society lose its moral balance. Nehru, who was personally close to Gandhiji and ideologically close to Tagore, saw more value in the modern state than they did in providing a unifying structure in a divided society and in unleashing the forces of planned economic development.

By the time the Indian Constitution was framed, both Gandhiji and Tagore were dead. Nehru (along with Ambedkar), in leading the way, drew upon the society-centric pluralistic idea of nationalism of Gandhiji and Tagore and gave it a legal-juridical form in the Indian Constitution. The Nehru-Ambedkar idea of nationalism, forged and refined through elaborate deliberations of the Constituent Assembly, gave India the basis of its civic nationalism that prevailed for many decades.

It is this inclusive idea of civic nationalism that is now being attempted to be dismantled by the Hindu nationalists. Even at the time of the framing of the Constitution, the RSS had opposed the Constitution as 'western', even though in their earlier history, many of their leaders used to admire the ethnic basis of nationalism in a western country, Germany—their revered leaders like Savarkar and Golwalkar had expressed open admiration for the efficient Nazi system of mobilising and organising the German nation. Earlier, Japanese nation-state had also been inspired by German history. It is not surprising that Tagore's lectures in Japan as early as 1916 against the aggrandising nation-state did not make him popular with the Japanese.

In the West, the US is a case where the idea of civic nationalism was pursued (though not always successfully). In a 2009 speech, Barack Obama said: 'One of the great strengths of the United States is . . . we do not consider ourselves a Christian nation, (but) a nation of citizens who are bound by ideals and a set of values', presumably as enshrined in the Constitution. This is a major historical example of what the

German philosopher Habermas calls 'constitutional patriotism', as opposed to patriotism based on 'blood and soil' which used to have popular appeal in Germany, and which in history has been associated with a great deal of persecution, violence and devastation. It is this German history that Einstein may have had in mind when he said nationalism is 'an infantile disease, the measles of mankind'.

This battle of alternative versions of nationalism is raging all over the world today. Our identities are necessarily multi-layered but ethnic nationalists privilege one of these layers, usually based on the narrow particularities of religion, language or culture that makes it easy to mobilise certain groups. In the name of national integration and fighting enemies, both outside and within, they undermine minority rights and procedures of democracy, they accuse liberals of appeasing the minorities (blacks and Hispanics in the US, immigrants in Europe, Kurds in Turkey, Muslims in India), and try to suppress dissent as 'anti-national'. Civic nationalism, on the other hand, emphasises the procedural aspects of democracy, and through its stress on liberal constitutional values tries to use the pre-commitment of a foundational document to bind the hands of subsequent generations against majoritarian tendencies curbing basic civil rights. If we lose this ideological battle in India, the foundational values of our multi-cultural society that our earlier great social thinkers adored will be in serious danger.

Economic Policy Issues, Going Forward

Economic Times, 5 August 2019

Now that elections are over, no one in the ruling dispensation needs to pretend that the economy has not been in dire doldrums for quite some time. There are many severe problems the economy faces, some requiring immediate attention, others more structured long-term policy changes. Of the former, I'll pick two.

First is the continuing scourge of demand deficiency (and the resultant low capacity utilisation) that discourages private investment. More than tinkering with tax concessions or interest rates, one needs pump priming public investment on a large scale. The lack of investment is associated with lack of non-farm jobs and massive underemployment and unemployment, particularly among our restless youth (providing the foot soldiers of gangster-politicians and lynch-mobs).

So, the public investment has to be job-creating—in construction, roads, public housing, warehouses, cold storage, etc. In rural areas, demand has to be boosted through more such construction programmes and by expanding the scale of National Rural Employment Guarantee Act (NREGA) schemes. It's not really 'employment guarantee', as evidence suggests that there is a large unmet demand for such jobs in many states.

Evidence also suggests that leakages in the original programme have now diminished substantially. This rural programme now needs to be supplemented by an urban employment guarantee on public works and civic programmes improving our crumbling urban infrastructure.

So, where will the money come from, at a time when fiscal deficit is rising? With relatively low inflation, we may afford to relax a bit on the fiscal deficit goals if money is productively spent on income-boosting construction and capital projects. Besides, India's tax-GDP ratio has remained low and stagnant even after decades of high growth, while wealth inequality (as measured by National Sample Survey) has now mounted to almost South American levels.

A large-scale reform of our current subsidies (much of which are enjoyed by the rich and middle-classes), and increase in direct taxes (with current under-taxation of property values and capital gains and zero-taxation of wealth, inheritance and agricultural incomes) can be carried out at a relatively short notice.

The other looming problem we can't look away from any more is the water crisis—for both drinking water and irrigation in large parts of water-depleted and ecologically stressed India. Along with immediate and drastic reduction of power and water subsidies, mass mobilisation of decentralised water-user associations in water management and rainfall harvesting is imperative. Of the more long-run policy issues, let me flag only a few. Our whole secondary education system has to be largely restructured and channelled to a mass-scale vocational training programme, in partnership with private employers.

Otherwise, many jobseekers will remain unemployable. In view of our dismal export performance—at a time when Vietnam is picking up the sectors China is graduating from— and the slump in our job-creating automobile and ancillary sectors, renewed efforts at a coordinated industrial policy, particularly in financing and supportive regulatory environment, are urgent.

In agriculture, where there is a large potential for job-creation in high-valued produce like fruit, vegetables and livestock products, what is needed, apart from investment in rural infrastructure, is opening up all marketing channels, thus disabling the current cartelised markets, and facilitating the widespread formation of farm companies and cooperatives to stem the adverse effects of declining land size.

The largely wasteful and iniquitous current minimum support price (MSP) policy should be oriented mainly towards millet crops and pulses. All this will require political courage. But that should not be beyond the capacity of our current muscular leadership.

In a country with one of the world's largest disease burdens, Government of India (GoI) is pushing Ayushman Bharat, an underfunded and hyped programme of insurance for hospital indoor expenditure for the poor. In general, India has yet to debate seriously at the political level why a subsidised private insurance model to cover only about 40% of the population—and that too not for their more substantial expenses on drugs and outdoor visits—is to be preferred to other models of universal healthcare with larger risk pools bringing down costs (as, say, in Thailand or Australia).

A large number of Indians, even far above the poverty line, face all kinds of brutal weather, health or market-related risks in life.

To provide some minimum economic security against such risks—apart from boosting the autonomy of women in the family and the fallback option of all informal workers—unconditional basic income supplement for everybody, far beyond PM-KISAN for farmers, should be implemented in phases.

Finally, administratively, we are retreating from effective decentralisation needed for successful economic policy in a large diverse country. Power remains over-concentrated in the PMO, choking decision points, while Bills impinging on state powers are hurriedly passed in the Parliament without consulting the states. All this is making a mockery of the oft-repeated rhetoric of 'cooperative federalism'.

Political loyalty and seniority, rather than performance, dictate promotion of bureaucrats, and public sector enterprises and regulatory bodies for private sector operations remain 'independent' only on paper.

From Democracy to Some Form of Thugocracy

Indian Express, 18 January 2020

Contrary to expectation in many quarters five years back, the current regime has proved itself rather inept and incompetent in economic policy matters, partly because of over-centralisation of power with dependence on loyal mediocrities for policy advice, and partly because for a long time, it believed in its own hype and was in denial.

Today large masses of our farmers remain in long-term agrarian and ecological distress, growing numbers of our burgeoning young population do not have anywhere near what can be called good jobs, much of the non-farm economy remains stalled by the slump in private investment and debt overhang and our exports remain uncompetitive in the world market. Meanwhile, corruption in the form of crony capitalism and murky election-funding (including the dubious device of electoral bonds) continues, never mind the empty rhetoric we had heard around demonetisation, which in effect turned out to be largely an assault on India's poor in the informal sector. Yet such was the magic of propaganda that many in the electorate believed in that rhetoric at that time, just as in 2019 large parts of the electorate went along with the leaders' call for 'dedicating' their votes to the Balakot airstrike (even though the pesky foreign press kept on finding the strike to be largely a fizzle, if not a hoax). In any case, it is a sad commentary on the inferiority complex in our national consciousness that we feel great as a nation by such an airstrike on a hapless unenviable neighbouring country, which so obsesses our politicians that they fail to see that today we are behind our other neighbours like Bangladesh and Sri Lanka in many socio-economic indicators, not to speak of our towering northern neighbour, China.

As the economy tanks, the incentive for our rulers to divert public attention with divisive Hindu-nationalist antics gets stronger. So, Kashmir loses its state rights, Kashmiris lose their civil rights, effectively anti-Muslim citizenship laws are rammed through the legislature, and all kinds of changes to rights to information or to dissident opinion or even the definition of who is to be called a terrorist are launched. In the name of democracy, majoritarian minority-baiting Hindu nationalists are rampaging all around—these are in a way the step-children of Jinnah, who also believed in the religious basis of nationalism, something Gandhiji fought against much of his political life. All this is regularly cheered on by a largely spineless or intimidated media.

The ruling party is confident in carrying out these excesses on the basis of a supposedly democratic mandate that they think their 'landslide' electoral majority (with 37 per cent of the vote) has given them. India today is the world's largest pretend-democracy, sadly but steadily creeping from democracy to some form of thugocracy. In the last more than two centuries of world democracy, what has been regarded as the essential kernel of democracy is not so much in the winning of elections as in protecting minority rights. As early as 1787, James Madison, a founding father of the American Constitution, made it clear in Federalist Papers that the central concern of democracy really lies in protecting citizens against the tyranny of the majority. Civic, as opposed to religious, nationalist founders of the American and the Indian Constitution thus emphasised various institutional checks and balances and separation of powers to protect minority rights and due process.

One by one these institutions are being decimated in India (the process started earlier, but it has been substantially accelerated under the current regime). The judiciary, which is supposed to guard against this, is timid, erratic, and sometimes, compromised. The police and the bureaucracy are complicit—in fact the police often join the majoritarian lynch-mobs in their mayhem (there are stories that the 'termites' from the Sangh Parivar have been quietly eating at the vitals of some these institutions from inside for some time). In India's largest state, police brutalities against and 'encounter killings' of minorities have become routine. The investigative agencies and tax administrators are allegedly harassing, raiding, and persecuting people deemed to be in opposition to the government. The increased extortionary powers of these agencies have multiplied opportunities for official corruption.

One of the insulating structures in the Constitution (more in the American than the Indian) against centralised abuse of power was that of federalism. For far too long, even the opposition states have allowed the central government to usurp powers arbitrarily, to assault the basic structure of the Constitution in many ways, violate the spirit of federalism in not involving or consulting the state governments while ramming through crucial legislations on policing, law and order, and social welfare services (all of which constitutionally are state subjects), in changing the terms of reference of the constitutional body of Finance Commission, in letting Niti Aayog to be merely a central government mouthpiece and the Inter-State Council to be in hibernation, and so on.

Even when the central government actions are technically legal, one can follow Gandhiji who had taught Indians to organise mass non-violent civil disobedience when the laws are not socially legitimate. It is a matter of some hope that there are now some flickering lights in this respect all over the country in the surrounding darkness.

Growth vs Hindutva Challenge

Times of India, 21 January 2016*

One of the campaign promises of the BJP was to end the scams of the UPA. Has corruption significantly declined since the BJP government came to power?

Even ignoring the current scams in Madhya Pradesh, Chhattisgarh and elsewhere, it's a little superficial to think that corruption has decreased since this government came to power, because the structural reasons for corruption remain. A few years back we used to hear about the mining mafia, we don't hear about it that much now. This is largely because the prices of minerals have gone down globally and political allocation of mineral and other natural resources doesn't make much money anymore. So the decline of the resource-related scams has little to do with the Modi government. Election expenses are an important structural source of corruption. The ruling party spent a staggeringly large amount of money (collected one presumes from the corporate sector) in the last national election (2014) and there must be a payback some time. Also, a lot depends on what we call 'corruption'. Cronyism is also a form of corruption. This government, like the previous one, gives huge tax concessions and other favours

---

* An Interview with Sagarika Ghose

to the corporate sector, a sort of corporate dole, often to politically-connected business groups.

Also when the main monitoring agency for corruption, the Central Bureau of Investigation (CBI), is subject to political manipulation, how can corruption be checked? In China, local officials are promoted on the basis of how well the local economies under them perform. There's thus an in-built check against stealing too much because if the local economy suffers, officials don't get promoted. In India, officials are promoted according to seniority, so there's no check on looting. Structural reform in administration is important if you want to end corruption.

Cooperative federalism is a buzz word of this government, is it working well?

Cooperative federalism is a catchy slogan but there's not yet enough to go by. The last Finance Commission moved in the right direction providing for more of tax proceeds going to states. However, earnings from central cesses like the Swachh Bharat cess and the education cess are not shared with the states. Also, schemes which were earlier sponsored by the Centre have been pushed to the states so their expenditure liabilities have gone up. In the midst of talk of devolution of power, there seems to be more centralisation of authority in the PMO than ever before. Before the Bihar elections of 2015 when Modi announced in a public meeting a large special package for Bihar with an auction-style drama, without consulting the state officials, that is cooperative federalism Modi-style.

There was a feeling that the Planning Commission was distributing money arbitrarily but its replacement the Niti Aayog has no power to distribute such money. Such monies are now allocated by the Finance Ministry. How is this federalism? Niti Aayog is just another think tank; its financial allocation powers have been taken away, which is why many chief ministers don't take it too seriously. Also, most decisions about the so-called smart cities are being taken centrally, states are hardly involved.

Your overall assessment of the economic policies of the Modi government?

Lots of catchy slogans, the PM is an excellent spin master but follow-ups do not match the dramatic initial gestures. Some schemes with new names are simply continuations to earlier programmes, as in streamlining of subsidies, direct benefit schemes, Aadhaar and coal auctions. Swachh Bharat is a continuation to Nirmal Bharat and the unexamined issue is, why many toilets built under the earlier programme were not used. There are several questions here, including the important one of Hindu cultural taboos about toilet cleaning.

The biggest problem to me is that this government came to power on the promise of creating jobs, which has hardly been kept so far. You see, the so-called 'Gujarat model' is a high growth model but it's not a job-creating model. Much of growth in Gujarat was in petrochemicals, petroleum refineries and pharmaceuticals; those are highly capital-intensive or skill-intensive. They do not give jobs to the relatively uneducated unskilled vast numbers of India's youth.There's not been much follow through on the jobs front, despite Make in India, Skill India, etc.

So, who is winning Bhagwat or Bhagwati?

There is a kind of division of labour in the new regime between RSS and its ex-pracharak PM. Incremental economic reform (some of it a continuation of the policies of the UPA regime) will not be objected to by the populist-nationalists in the RSS, as long as the latter are given a free hand in controlling the agenda of education, culture and history. The Dinanath Batraisation of textbooks (in effect distorting history and poisoning the minds of young people) continues, which is the long-lasting damage. In India, there's always been an unhealthy amount of state control over education and culture, but the current regime has mobilised an unusually large number of bigots and charlatans for this job. In general, the average competence level of ministers in this government is quite low (compared, say, even to Vajpayee's government). Bhagwat and Bhagwati exist in tandem. If the economy doesn't do well, and young people get frustrated, they can always ratchet up the cultural stuff—cows, 'love jihad', beef, and the rest of it.

There was a surge in the creation of bank accounts for the poor a few years back when NREGA wages started being paid into bank accounts. The Jan Dhan Yojana is more vigorous, but will not mean much as long as the accounts remain dormant. Budget cutting and inordinate delay in wage payments are slowly smothering NREGA.

What the Modi Government Has—and Hasn't—Done So Far

The Wire, 26 July 2016*

What would you say are the economic reasons for the anti-establishment political forces we've seen coming up, from different sides of the political spectrum, in the US and Europe?

There are many things happening in the world, but the ones I suppose you are referring to are the recent, unexpected rise of (Donald) Trump in the US, the triumph of Brexit in Britain and in general, the rise of a lot of right-wing parties in Europe. Everybody is saying that there are several factors involved.

One is the consequence of globalisation. From globalisation, a lot of people have benefited. Certainly owners of capital have benefited, owners of technology have benefited. People like you and me who are more flexible because of our education and can move around the world, we have also benefited from globalisation. Even some poor people, like the young women in the garment export industry in Bangladesh, have benefited. But many other members of the working class have not, particularly in Europe and the US. A lot of workers in manufacturing industry have lost their jobs because many of

---

*   An Interview

the industries have moved production to China and other countries. So those workers are dissatisfied and it is not an accident that both in Britain and in the US they have expressed their sympathy for those kind of causes. So that's one factor—globalisation. Not just globalisation, the unequal benefits flowing from globalisation.

Second, even if globalisation were not there, this tremendous technical change that's going on has to be reckoned with. Globalisation has also interacted with technology, but even if there was no globalisation, technological change would have caused job losses of various kinds. That would have increased dissatisfaction, particularly of workers who do not have much skill or education to take advantage of the new technology. So there's dissatisfaction because of that. Automation, for example. In the West, already robots are taking away jobs in some sectors. Robots can easily take jobs in relatively routine type of work. That's why many unskilled workers who are losing out are worried. That's factor number two.

Factor number three. For quite some time, for various reasons including the first two reasons that I mentioned, labour movements in the world are getting weaker. By labour movements I particularly mean those led by trade unions. Trade unions are getting weaker, so as a result labour is struggling. Workers' causes have suffered. There are not that many movements taking up the cause of the disgruntled worker, that's factor number three.

Factor number four, which is very important in the US and Western Europe, is immigration. Even if these other factors were not there, just because of immigration, there would have been discontent. Immigration is related to globalisation in some sense. Globalisation is free movement of goods, free movements of people, free movements of capital—of these the free movement of people is immigration. And immigration has this special issue, which may not be in the first three factors that I mentioned. For the first three factors that I mentioned, their effects are largely economic. The fourth, immigration, is not just economic. Of course, immigration has economic consequences but it also affects cultural relations and the social fabric. Quite often, local people do not like (whether for right or wrong reasons) the new culture that the immigrants are bringing—new religious beliefs, morals and cultural practices, for example those with respect to women and to liberal values in general. So that causes some resentment. And the other issue related to culture is that the old community bonds of those societies are frayed.

I think if you combine these four factors, there is a lot of disgruntlement particularly among the poor and particularly among the older people. Older people voted largely for Brexit, for instance. Of course, in numbers the older people vote more than the young so it comes out in the votes much more. But older workers who are used to some types of technology, culture and social issues feel threatened. Also, younger people can adjust more easily to take different types of jobs, older people don't have that. Those, I think, are the fundamental factors behind this phenomenon.

And would you say this disgruntlement is a serious threat to mainstream economic orthodoxy?

As I said, it's not just economic, it's cultural and social too. The answer to your question would depend on what you mean by economic orthodoxy. If you mean by economic orthodoxy the idea that free movement of goods and capital is good, obviously this is against that. However, there's a different aspect of orthodoxy, what you would call macroeconomic orthodoxy, and this is a matter of the big dispute in the West. The economic orthodoxy which emphasises restraining the government and the macroeconomic policy of austerity. If you regard Keynesianism as non-orthodoxy (in some contexts Keynesian policy is already a part of the orthodoxy), that is a big dispute. Countries which have taken the policy of austerity have not been successful in creating jobs. So obviously this increases disgruntlement.

The other thing is, and I don't know if you can call it orthodoxy or not, in many Western countries, macroeconomic policy that gets prominence is monetary policy, interest rate policy. In a sense, Keynesians say that monetary policy is not enough, we have to do fiscal expansion, etc. But fiscal expansion means also raising more taxes and that is what the right-wing quite often in the US and in Europe are resisting. So those disputes are related to the economic orthodoxy issue.

To move a little bit to the specifics of India, since 1991, India has been going in a certain direction in terms of economic policy. Would you say this has been good for the country? Also, would you say there's been some difference in economic policy between the Congress and the BJP, or in the way they package their policies?

I'll not have a simple answer to this. Do I support the movement towards economic liberalisation that started with the delicensing in the mid-1980s, my general answer is yes. Because when don't allow market forces to work, and this used to be true for the licence permit raj, what happens is that those licences and permits go to only some politically favoured groups like the case of earlier licences and permits mainly going to the monopoly business houses. I am generally in favour of opening up of opportunities for more people. It is also important that this economic liberalisation has coincided with a social phenomenon in India, which is often not commented on. It is also in this period that through democracy, gradually the lower castes and in general the weaker sections of the population (of course only some of them not all of them) have been able to come up and benefit from these new opportunities.

I'll give you an example. Particularly in South India and West India, peasant castes (not the really low but in the middle ranks) became gradually not only more economically prosperous, but in general socially more assertive. Take the case of garment industry around Coimbatore; the main entrepreneurs there are often from a caste group called Gounder, a peasant caste. They did well in agriculture, got some money and they invested the money in this. These are not from established business houses like Tatas, Birlas and Ambanis, they are the new entrepreneurs.

So I'm just saying along with economic liberalisation, this has been a period in which some limited amount of social transformation has occurred, largely because of our democracy. So these new entrepreneurs have been able to take opportunities opened up by liberalisation. A lot of people say there are a lot more even Dalit entrepreneurs now, but one should not exaggerate. The phenomenon is observable more for the middle castes.

So, in general my answer is yes, but that does not mean I am wholeheartedly in favour of liberalisation, unless some corrective measures are taken to curb its adverse effects. Everybody would recognise that when you open up markets, just as opportunities open up for people, the benefits are unequally distributed, particularly because initial endowments and available social and infrastructural facilities are different for different people. So yes, I gave you some examples of lower groups coming up, but in general, inequality has been increasing all over the world, including in India. So market reform has to be accompanied with measures to correct those inequalities.

That's where the Congress-BJP issues come up, because I think in the UPA I regime, in the 2004-2009 period, there were some attempts in response to this problem of inequality, some efforts were taken to improve welfare of common people. The National Advisory Council (NAC) that Sonia Gandhi created had some effect. For example, NREGA, the rural employment guarantee, came in that period pushed by the NAC, even though the idea of employment on public works as a safety net for poor people is quite old in India. Similarly, a very important measure was the Right to Information Act, 2005.

That also grew out of a movement which was there earlier. The Scheduled Tribes and Other Traditional Forest Dwellers (Recognition of Forest Rights) Act, 2006, which by the way is yet to be fully implemented, came as a way to stop the long dispossession of tribal people from their land and rights to use forests.

These are, in a way, in reaction to forces of inequality generated by market reform. So you might say those are positive aspects of the UPA regime. But there are many negative aspects of the UPA regime too. But let me go on to the BJP. Has BJP taken different policies? I think BJP's difference in these matters is often more in rhetoric than in actuality. BJP, has not got rid of the programmes that I just mentioned. Even though they were very much opposed to NREGA, it's ironical that the BJP is now taking credit for it. So that's good. Earlier Modi came out with lot of things against NREGA, saying that 'we'll keep it as a monument to the failures of the Congress'. And now his ministers are claiming credit for that. That doesn't mean that everything is fine with NREGA, there's still lot of corruption and leakage in NREGA. The government is not helping matters, as in many cases, I understand that wage payments have not been made for several months. This is very serious, not only because it is hurting the poor. The whole idea of NREGA is that if I as a landless worker demand work, the government guarantees work. If I find that when I work, I'm not paid for six months, the next time I will not demand work. So in a sense there is a self-fulfilling aspect to its failure. In any case, it is not true that wherever work was demanded, it was given. There's a lot of unmet wants in NREGA. There are a lot of other problems in NREGA, but even with all that I would say NREGA has been a major positive step in India.

Similarly, the other thing that the UPA regime did which BJP has not discontinued is the National Food Security Act (NFSA), 2013, which now in rural areas is to reach around 75% of the people. In fact, people have not commented on this—

in West Bengal, I find, on of the platforms on which Mamata Banerjee won was the programme of Rs 2 per kg of rice. That was very popular. What Mamata never mentioned, and I'm surprised opposition didn't mention much either, is that this is part of the central government scheme. Mamata expanded on it a little bit, but it is largely an impact of the Act.

In general, I would say on many of these welfare measures which UPA started, BJP, whatever the rhetoric, has more or less continued. I would not say that there is a big difference.

One difference for BJP I should comment on here. Modi in the 2014 elections, said that we have to have a new approach. The UPA approach was 'giving doles', he said. We're going to create jobs instead, so that is a different approach. First of all, he has not created enough jobs and I don't think by 2019 the job situation is going to change very much, I don't expect much of a dent on the enormous and alarming problem of not enough good jobs for the young people. The other day, in one interview Mr Modi has said, yes jobs are being created, but they're as yet invisible. We have a whole statistical machinery, very soon these jobs should have been captured in the statistics! We don't see that. In fact, the Labour Bureau now collects a few times every year job data for eight industries, eight relatively labour-intensive industries. And, if you look at them, if anything it's getting worse. So where are Mr Modi's invisible jobs?

This new approach of job creation, I think it was basically a hoax on the electorate. The BJP before coming to power gave the impression that 'we are going to create jobs, look at the Gujarat model'. The Gujarat model is not a model for creating jobs! Gujarat is a state where the economic growth rate was high, but not necessarily job creation. Economic growth rate was high partly because Modi as chief minister gave a lot of capital subsidies to the large companies, run by the Ambanis, Adanis, and Essar. They are primarily in capital-intensive industries like petrochemicals, petroleum refineries, etc. And, if you disaggregate Gujarat's growth, a large part of the growth was in these sectors. So Gujarat is a model of high growth but not of jobs. These two have been mixed up in the election campaign in 2014.

But going back to doles, just now I told you that Modi's model, the Gujarat model, was based on capital subsidies. What is that? That's dole to the capitalists. Even on a national level if you look at the data and check how much of our subsidies go to the better off people, it's a very substantial sum. In fact, there are some estimates which show that of our total subsidies that the government gives both in the Centre and the states, the amounts that go to the better off exceed 10% of GDP. So why do you object to doles to the poor when you are giving a much larger amount to the wealthy (a few times larger than our total anti-poverty programmes)? Modi or anybody has no ground to stand on when they talk disparagingly about doles to the poor.

What would you say the government could be doing differently in terms of employment generation and anti-poverty programmes?

Employment generation is a very difficult subject. Employment is not that easy to generate, that's why I'm pessimistic about the prospects. Yes, there are some things that can be done in the long run. For example, suppose you are a small producer. Like the majority of producers in India you are in the informal sector, you have a little shop, a little household enterprise. So what are your main problems? Main problems are quite often things like electricity. Suppose you are in the garment industry, which is highly labour-intensive and creates lots of jobs. At the moment you employ say 5-6 people, an informal household enterprise. Now you are thinking of expanding to hire 50 people.

Quite often in India it is said, jobs are not being created because of labour laws. Because in India, the labour laws tell you that if you hire more than 100 people and if you want to sack somebody, you need government permission. So that restricts hiring. But let me go back to this concrete example. This guy who was hiring 5-6 people now is thinking of expanding to 50, labour law is not a problem. Labour law kicks in when you have 100, right?

When I'm thinking of expanding to hire 50 people, a little larger size, what are my binding constraints? Electricity is a major one, because at the moment the only use of electricity I probably have is a little light bulb. Now, maybe I will need tailoring machines or other kinds of power equipments. So then I have to worry about whether I have a regular supply of electricity. Even if I have regular supply, does the voltage fluctuate? With voltage fluctuations these machines are going to burn out. So those issues to me are concrete issues. So what we do about electricity is very important.

To be fair to Mr Modi, he's done a good job about electricity in Gujarat. But now that he's Prime Minister of India, he has to do it to the rest of India. I've not seen many signs of that. Electricity reform, to me, is a very important part of reform, which neither UPA nor the current administration has done much about. Electricity is a major input needed for people to expand jobs. Many people regard UDAY, the programme the government has introduced for financial restructuring of the heavily-losing state electricity distribution companies is more like 'kicking the can down the road'.

Similarly, roads. Roads improve connectivity. I understand that one of the areas in which this government has done reasonably well is in building roads. I hope that continues. So in the long run electricity and roads are extremely important for creating jobs, much more important in my judgement than labour laws. If labour laws are reformed, I have nothing against it. But I don't think that is a major constraint. That is one of 20 other constraints. But people give too much emphasis on labour reform.

There's something that I would suggest for employment generation in the short run, which I don't find people suggesting. Currently, in order to encourage investment, the government gives subsidies to capitalists. So essentially you come with your capital and you'll get a subsidy, a tax holiday or other facilities in a Special Economic Zone, these are all parts of capital subsidies. When you subsidise capital, it is not a surprise that people will use capital-intensive technology and not many jobs will be created. So that immediately suggests to me an opposite policy, wage subsidy. Why don't you start a policy that says to the capitalists, if you create more jobs instead of introducing automation, machines etc, for each new person you hire, the wage that you have to pay will be subsidised by the government. To me, there is a great deal of scope for converting at least a part of the large capital subsidies into wage subsidies.

In our country now bulging with young people, the employment situation is potentially a big social problem. Already in parts of India it's happening. In West Bengal, I see this all the time. In fact, in West Bengal if you get a car and drive around the state, you'll be stopped in many places. Young people will come and stop your car and say you have to pay money. They will of course tell you 'this puja, that puja' etc. It's just that they don't have jobs, essentially they're collecting their forms of taxes. This will happen more and more in other parts of North India. In large parts of West Bengal now, if you want to build, you have to buy materials from these particular young people who will charge a much higher price and for inferior material. Otherwise, *gundas* will come and not allow you to build. So where are these people coming from? As they don't have jobs, they are into criminal and semi-criminal occupations.

On poverty alleviation, I'm in general in support of many of the poverty alleviation policies. NREGA, I am very much in support of. But, there are some subsidies I'm against; I think I'm in general in favour of phasing out the fertiliser subsidies which is at the moment is costly financially and environmentally. Similarly, I'd in general phase out the policy of support prices given to producing rice and wheat. Rice is a water-intensive crop which is often grown in unsuitable areas (like Punjab), depleting the water table. The other thing it is doing, apart from damaging the environment and costing a great deal of money, it focuses attention on two cereals—rice and wheat. Agriculture has to diversify, we should go much more into fruits, vegetables and dairy products, livestock products in general. One constraint that we have is that for products like fruits, vegetables, dairy and livestock products, we need cold storage. So I would suggest lot more investment in cold storage and roads.

If in India if you can reduce large parts of what I called before the subsidies to the better off, you'll be able to give what is called a basic income to everybody. In my scheme, any citizen of India will get, every month, a certain amount of money, no questions asked. I have made calculations that if the subsidies to the better off are given up in India, then you can afford to give every person in India Rs 10,000 a year. If you have a family of four, that's Rs 40,000. That's a big change to poverty. You don't need fresh taxation; the only thing you need is to get rid of the subsidies to the better off. But suppose, in the beginning you cannot get rid of all the subsidies to the better off, well get rid of as many as you can but meanwhile you need taxes. I think there's great deal of taxable capacity in our real estate sector. The real estate sector is a sector in which values are off and on going up in every city, even small cities. But the government is not getting enough out of it, much of it going into the so-called black economy.

One area in which I would say both the UPA regime and particularly the Modi regime is guilty of not doing anything is health. This is big deficiency of Indian policy.

People often do not know that in health expenditure, India is not just third world but fourth world. India's health expenditure as proportion of GDP is lower than in many other poor nations. Secondly, most of the expenditure is not in public health. Most of the diseases in India are because of public health and sanitation problems. That's where the emphasis should be. The Swachh Bharat campaign for sanitation (which is a continuation to the UPA Nirmal Bharat Abhiyan) concentrates on toilet building through contractors, without looking into why the toilets are often malfunctioning, why they are not used by many. The issues of public education towards better habits of personal hygiene can be handled better by social activists and NGOs than by bureaucrats, but this government is unduly suspicious of NGOs in general. Thirdly, there was some talk in the last few days of the UPA regime and the first few days of the Modi regime of a move towards universal health care. I find now the Modi government is going in the opposite direction. There is a Niti Aayog document suggesting that we go away from universal healthcare towards subsidised private health insurance. That's the US model—a highly defective and prohibitively expensive model. This is not the right model for us. Of course, it is not easy to construct a service like the National Health Service in the UK or a similar system in France. But you don't have to look to UK or France. A neighbouring country, Thailand, now has a universal health service. Study that case and see what they have done. It's not that expensive to do. In health, it seems like we're going in the opposite direction.

In the Indian context that we've been talking about with the critical employment problem and increasing inequality, what do you make of initiatives like Make in India or Smart Cities?

I'm not as enthusiastic as the current government is about the Smart Cities programme. If there are no other constraints then it's okay, but it seems to me that most of the emphasis in the Smart Cities programme is on digitisation, IT etc. But most of our cities are not liveable at the moment. Make it liveable for the majority of the population that is where the real smartness lies, digitisation is not the real smartness.

Make in India, I'm not even sure what it means. If Make in India means something should be produced in India, not elsewhere, that goes back to the old protectionist regime. If that is the case then I'm not sure I'm in favour of it. But in general, if you want to encourage manufacturing, I'm all for it. There are many constraints, I've already mentioned some kinds of constraints. For Make in India, you need a great deal of reform in electricity and other infrastructural facilities. You also need a great deal of private and public investment.

At the moment, there is a big stagnation going on in private investment because of the bank debt problem. Wilful defaulters have not paid back huge loans, so the banks are in trouble. Therefore, the banks don't want to lend, so there is a debt overhang and stagnation in the field of private investment in India now. This means all the more that public investment has to go up. The problem with public investment is twofold. One is where is the money going to come from? Now I would not be against even increasing fiscal deficit to spend on public investment, but there both the UPA government and the current government have an external problem. They're worried that international credit rating agencies will lower our rating if the deficit increases. Now what is the cost of lowering rating? A lot of portfolio investment by foreign financial institutions will suffer. But I am not sure this volatile part of foreign investment should be encouraged. It may also affect FDI. But as yet foreign investment is not coming to fields which will create many jobs. So I think I'd worry less about foreign investment. I'm generally in favour of foreign investment, but not at the expense of domestic public investment. So that's one problem.

The other problem is that for quite some time, we have followed the mode of public private partnership (PPP), that did not work. In fact, in many cases there has been corruption in PPP. The whole modality of PPP has to be re-thought, has to be made transparent and less corruption prone. There is a tendency, whenever one thinks about reforming PPP, that when the business is doing well, private people make money, but when it's not, there is pressure for renegotiation of terms and the losses are on the public sector. This peculiar principle—privatise the profit and socialise the losses is not the way to run a PPP. So I think PPPs, which otherwise I'm in favour of because the government does not have enough money, has to be re-thought of and reorganised.

One of the other big things that Modi talked a lot about in his campaign was federalism and increasing power to the states. But a lot of people have argued that in his tenure what he has actually done is increase centralisation. Would you agree with that?

I largely agree. Everybody knows that power has been centralised into PMO, the Prime Minister's Office. In fact, that has sometimes made difficult to make quick decisions, which goes against two of the government's objectives, that of easing business and of federalism.

Similarly, before the Bihar elections, Modi went to a big election rally in the state and announced a special package for Bihar and the way he went about it was very interesting. In front of thousands of people, he said how much money will be given to Bihar (without any consultation with Bihar officials). He said, '50,000 crore! *Nahi*, 80,000 crore! *Nahi*, 1,20,000 crore!' It was like a public auction. This is not federalism. This is what I call 'federalism Modi-style'. To me it's the king giving largess to his subjects. But more substantially, yes some money has been transferred to the states. But that is not Modi's doing, that has been done by the Finance Commission, which is a constitutional body, and its dispensations are constitutionally mandated for the government to follow, whether it be Modi or anyone else.

Another to notice, also true for the UPA regime, is that in recent years, in the budget, there are a lot of new cesses. Education cess, Swachh Bharat cess, etc. An interesting thing about a cess is that you don't have to share it with the states. This is not good for federal finance.

And lastly, one institution which could have played a creative role in federalism is the Niti Aayog. Now the problem with Niti Aayog as I see it is that unlike the Planning

Commission, it does not have any financial powers. Planning Commission could at least decide how much money states would get for some centrally-sponsored schemes, so chief ministers used to take it seriously. But now that power has been given to the finance ministry. So that is centralisation, not decentralisation. So the Niti Aayog has mainly policy suggestions powers, no financial powers, and therefore, many non-BJP chief ministers don't take Niti Aayog seriously. Second, in Niti Aayog meetings, discussions are usually held on an agenda preselected by the Central government, which do not suit the states. Third, if it is the job of Niti Aayog to coordinate with the states, there is already a pre-existing body called Inter-state Council which has been in existence since the 1990s. It did not meet for 10 years until recently. In fact, I have heard that officers posted in the Inter-state Council see it as a punishment posting, because nothing happens there. That's the organisation created to have inter-state coordination. I hope Niti Aayog postings don't get a similar reputation soon.

There is a debate among economists about how independent the central bank should be. If they are too independent, the charge is that they serve as the handmaiden of private banks and are not accountable to the people. But if they are not independent of government, it becomes hard for them to make tough decisions when those are sometimes needed. How should a country like India strike a balance, especially in the context of the controversy that Raghuram Rajan's tenure and imminent departure has triggered?

It's really sad about Raghuram Rajan, who is such a bright and wise person. India had a rare opportunity to have someone like him as the central banker, not many countries have this opportunity. We wasted this opportunity. Having RSS attack dogs out to get him and Mr Modi remaining silent, and opening his mouth to utter some platitudes only after Mr Rajan resigned—this is scandalous, in my judgement.

In Rajan's case something else may have happened. He was not very popular with the wilful defaulters on bank loans, many of whom are crony capitalists. I am sure from behind the scene they must have put pressure, because Rajan has come out with very strong strictures against them. He called them 'freeloaders', since it is essentially taxpayers money that they have taken and are defaulting on. I think that's also behind it, not just RSS pressure but also these tycoons and crony capitalists who were quite uncomfortable with the stringent policies Rajan was following.

I also find the current way of doing things problematic. There should be much more public debate and discussion on the issues and the different policy opinions of the candidates. But once you appoint, don't interfere. I am generally in favour of central bank independence subject not to day-to-day scrutiny but periodic review. Policies every 3-5 years should be discussed in public, in the Parliament, everywhere. But no day-to-day interference.

Rajan has recently come out with a statement that the governor's tenure should be at least five years, not three. I agree with that. But like I said, every three years, the Parliament and the public should have a discussion on the policies being followed in the last three years.

In any case, going back to something I mentioned before, there is too much focus on monetary policy. I think it should be much more balanced, both on fiscal and monetary policy. Our governments are always scared of what international credit rating agencies would think if they talk about fiscal expansion even for long-term investment.

Should India be seeking more trade and investment deals that integrate more fully with other economies? Should we focus on mega deals like TPP (Trans-Pacific Partnership) or the RCEP (Regional Comprehensive Economic Partnership) that is currently being negotiated or can they work against us?

Generally, I would say yes, India should integrate much more. These days, without integration you cannot succeed. It's not like the old days, when someone was good at producing something so they sell it in the world market. What has changed is the predominance of a global value chain. Different countries have different locations on the chain. If you can't find your own niche on the chain, then you've lost it. The Chinese have done a very good job at finding this niche and over time also moving up the ladder to higher value. They are now moving out of labour-intensive exports to more skill-intensive exports. So most laptops, smart phones, etc are now produced in China. We have no alternative but to integrate— become part of the global value chain.

That's my general principle. It's a different issue when it comes to the TPP or the RCEP. I'm not sure whether some of these trade agreements are helpful. TPP (Trans-Pacific Partnership) will probably help Vietnam, because they have many things to sell to the US. But I am not sure in general that the gain from TPP is that much. These deals vary from case to case.

What I don't like is that India, at the world forum, often takes a holier-than-thou economic-nationalist attitude. I don't think that's the right attitude. Then people laugh at us, they know India isn't a big power in the economic world. They can do without India. Even the one sector where we were big, the software sector, is now gradually going elsewhere, to the Philippines for instance, to Israel. So if it comes to that, the world might say okay go ahead, bye. We don't have that much bargaining power, so we shouldn't take that attitude.

Speaking of China, why do you think they have been able to grow so rapidly, move so many people out of agriculture and reduce poverty so much faster than India?

I have a book about this ('Awakening Giants, Feet of Clay: Assessing the Economic Rise of China and India', Princeton University Press, 2013). To give a two-minute answer, the Chinese have succeeded at something that we have not. And that goes back to something that I've mentioned before, about labour-intensive industrialisation. That's where poor people's jobs are. The reason we have a job problem is because we haven't solved this problem. We think of the IT sector, we think of Smart Cities—these aren't going to create jobs for poor people.

I also mentioned before the need for roads, electricity, etc to create jobs—this is where the Chinese's major success lies. Infrastructure is the major dazzling success in China. The first time I went to China was in 1989 and since then I go quite often. It's just breath-taking. And we are nowhere near that.

There are things that they can do that we can't do as easily. If they need to acquire land, they just do it immediately. We can't do that, there's a whole process. So there are things they can do because of the political system that we can't. But it's not just that. Going back to health and education, it's really tragic that India today is where China was in the early 1970s. Even before the reforms, during the Maoist period, they improved health and education immensely. As a result, Chinese workers are healthier and more educated than ours. That in itself increases productivity. Health and education should be improved no matter what, but Chinese workers are more productive simply because of these reasons. Secondly, is the physical infrastructure—roads, electricity, etc. Physical and social infrastructure together create a base for labour-intensive industrialisation. The groundwork was carried out in China in the socialist period and accelerated post-reform.

This area, social and physical infrastructure, I'd say is a major economic failure of India. And that has its effect on jobs and labour-intensive industrialisation. That has a substantial effect in reducing poverty.

Our poverty has also declined, but nothing like in China. They have raised above the poverty line nearly half a billion people within a short span of time.

Gujarat Model of Hate
is Evident Everywhere

The Telegraph, 22 January 2018*

PROMISES UNFULFILLED

Job Creation

This government came to power in 2014 by promising job creation. This, Modi described, was a departure from the UPA government's dole-driven regime. This was a winning slogan. We were also promised that the Gujarat model of development would be carried out in the rest of India. A promise was made to create 100 million new jobs by 2022, which appealed to the aspirational youth, particularly of North India. (As there has been a youth bulge in the demographics of the North Indian population, a large number of young people were fascinated by this promise.)

That the Gujarat model of high growth was not a particular exemplar in job creation did not deter the appeal. The Gujarat model, in spite of its high manufacturing growth, was particularly in sectors like petroleum refineries and petrochemicals, which are highly capital-intensive. They don't create that many jobs. The Gujarat model is neither an

---

*   Interview with Devadeep Purohit

exemplar in job creation nor in social welfare. Yet, it was used to appeal to the aspiration for jobs among the young people.

It is by now clear to many people that the pace of job creation has not been shining. In fact, some of the data—like the annual data produced by the Labour Bureau surveys—show that there may have been even some absolute decline in jobs. But this is not new. Even for the last 40 years, job growth in India has been by and large rather sluggish.

At the moment, some data suggest that we have a total number of workers exceeding 50 million who are either unemployed or underemployed. This doesn't count the hundreds of millions of women, who are outside the labour force. (In surveys, the surveyors ask question about employment to only those who are part of the labour force.)

Combating Corruption

Another big hoax is the regime's supposedly spectacular fight against corruption. After insignificant progress in getting the black money stashed in foreign accounts or from repeated announcements for tax amnesty, there was a sudden 'bold' launching of demonetisation in November 2016. This has turned out to be one of the grandest hoaxes ever in Indian political history.

The announced objective was to vaporise the corrupt cash hoarded by the rich. But then other objectives were also mentioned—to eliminate counterfeit money, to prevent terror funding. And when these things were not working, they talked about the need to digitise the economy. So, goalposts were changed over time.

Looking back now, we can say that most of the money has come back. This means that black money hoarded in the form of cash was tiny. Or, even if it was not tiny, it has been deftly returned through the backdoor with the complicity of corrupt bank officials.

Usually, most rich people do not keep their black money in cash. They use other means like real estate, gold, foreign account etc. I don't know what gave the government the idea that most black money was stashed in cash.

To this day, the hardship that it caused has not been properly measured. We, the urban middle class, all remember the long queues in front of the ATMs and our irritation with day-to-day changes in the regulations. But to me, what was done was a cruel joke on the Indian poor, particularly those in the informal sector. I think demonetisation was a hastily-thought-out programme by some ignorant but arrogant people in Delhi and foisted on an unprepared and somewhat confused bank bureaucracy.

We have now data—not for whole of India though—on the extent of losses in jobs and wages. Take the textile hubs like Panipat in North India and Tiruppur in South India. Now, there is evidence of huge losses in trading as well as jobs. We also have evidence of small companies losing out and the informal sector failing to pay wages and workers going back to their villages.

But the political magic of this hoax was that a majority of poor people believed that it was for punishing the corrupt rich. The poor did not realise that the rich did not suffer that much. Some people said that the real estate sector was hurt, but that's not correct. As the 2017 Economic Survey pointed out, real estate was down even before demoneti-sation was announced.

Some people said that tax returns increased because of demonetisation. But the same Economic Survey pointed out that the average income level of the new tax payers was Rs 2.7 lakh, slightly above the tax threshold. So, the new people brought under the tax net are not the superrich who have been evading tax all these years. They are more likely to be relatively small people who have come under the tax net because of pressure from the banks to link accounts with the Aadhaar card and the PAN card and the Goods and Services Tax (GST) bringing some people in. So, it is not that fat cats were disgorging their illicit hoards due to demonetisation.

PR COUPS

Clean Governance

The PR campaign that this regime is much cleaner is largely exaggerated. Let us ignore the gigantic Vyapam scam in the BJP regime in Madhya Pradesh in which 40 mysterious deaths of the witnesses and the accused had been reported. At least the scams in the UPA regime—take the 2G case—did not kill that many people. Then there is the cricket-related scams in Rajasthan and Delhi. Let's ignore that as well.

About the mineral and other natural resource related scams that were important under the UPA regime; I think today it is correct to say that the auctions of natural resources like minerals and coal are much cleaner. But they started to be cleaner towards the end of the UPA regime under the Supreme Court order. So, there is nothing new here. In any case, the international mining boom being over, there is now less money to be made in the mining sector.

Then, I should point out that attempts are reportedly being made to obstruct any action to be taken on the findings of the Directorate of Revenue Intelligence on the cases of large over-invoicing of power equipment and coal imports by some big corporate houses. Many stories about continuing corruption in government procurement, building and real estate deals and land grabs abound, but the CBI and the ED do not seem to be particularly keen to pursue these if they involve ruling party politicians.

As the intimidated NGOs and media largely keep quiet, you do not hear about these instances. At the level of everyday corruption, a recent survey—by the Centre for Media Studies—reports in 2017 that 43 per cent of households feel that the level of corruption has increased in the preceding year. This is petty corruption, something that households face in their day-to-day life.

Then, there is the elephant in the room—the matter of large election funding. Evidence suggests that the total donations to the ruling party are several times the donations to all the other parties combined.

All political parties are exempt from the RTI. But under what grounds? The political parties say they are not public entities. Now, if they are not public entities, they are private entities. Then, they must be NGOs or something like that. The NGOs are under the Foreign Contribution Regulation Act, and under that Act many NGOs are harassed these days.

Quietly in one of Arun Jaitley's Finance Bills, a clause had been added that made all political parties exempt from FCRA and it's retroactive to 2010. That means all the money that came for the 2014 elections cannot be investigated.

In the last budget, Jaitley introduced election bonds. This is really amazing. Under the new scheme of election bonds, corporate donations, practically without limits or without disclosure, can be made now. And the finance minister tells us, this will increase transparency. Exactly the opposite is the case.

The Lokpal Act—if anybody remembers that anymore—came to our statute books on 1 January 2014. Now it's January 2018. The BJP made a lot of hue and cry and pressed the UPA to pass the Lokpal Act. In the last four years, they did not find any time to either appoint a Lokpal or implement the Act. This follows a pattern. When Modi was the chief minister of Gujarat, in his more than 12 years' tenure, he did not get the time to appoint a Lokayukta.

Yet, the rhetoric of slaying of the demon of corruption continues in full force and many people swallow it. At the same time, the PM refuses to face public questions in media—I understand that he has not faced a single press conference—or questions in the Parliament. He has decided that one-way tweets and *Maan Ki Baat* radio talks are enough for the gullible.

REFORMIST APPROACH

Similarly, PR coup wise, GST was introduced with much fanfare at a midnight session of the Parliament and has been hailed as one of the biggest economic reforms in Indian history.

We are not supposed to remember that for quite some time, one of the main opponents of the original form of GST was a certain CM of Gujarat and now it is one of his major reforms. The PM has called it a 'good and simple tax'. It is interesting to remember that the version he had opposed as the CM was much better and simpler. Now because of the complexity of negotiations, it is no longer as good or as simple. This is part of the Indian political irony.

I am in favour of GST in general, but there are too many rates and too many exemptions—petroleum products and alcoholic beverages are outside its purview. I think it's a step in the right direction. The way it is implemented has been too hasty and clumsy, causing a great deal of hardship particularly to small business.

The government's approach to Aadhaar is another example of PR. The UPA regime was the architect of it and the BJP had strenuously opposed Aadhaar when it was in the Opposition. But the way it was introduced in the Lok Sabha—as a money bill—there could not be much discussion. There were serious things to be discussed like threat to privacy and data security. It is ominous that this was so hurriedly enacted and by a government that is quite trigger-happy with its powers of surveillance.

Even though in general one may be in favour of Aadhaar, one is hesitant about the way the whole thing has been implemented.

DIFFERENT PARTY

The last PR that I am going to talk about is the ruling party's success in creating an impression that it is a pan-Indian party rising above the narrow sectarian interests of caste, community and language that fragment Indian society. It also says it is above vote bank politics, unlike the Congress and the regional parties.

In reality, Amit Shah is busy forging very complex caste groupings and alliances. For example, in the Uttar Pradesh election, he very deftly crafted an alliance of non-Yadav and non-Jatav castes. The vote bank BJP nurses is the vote bank of Hindu supremacists. Language-wise, its linguistic practice, even in official transactions now, is of Hindi dominance.

The so-called nationalistic ideology that it propounds is not pan-Indian at all. It is highly exclusionary and based on a narrow sectarian concept of Hindi-Hindu-Hindustan. It pre-emptively brands any dissent from this narrowness as anti-national.

In fact, one may go to the other extreme and say that, in some respects, the Sangh *parivar* is more 'anti-national', as everyday they are violating, both in spirit and words, the ideal of civic nationalism based on the values embedded in our Constitution. I would go even one step further and say that they do not understand the Hindu philosophy as it has developed over thousands of years. Their 'Hindutva' is, in some sense, deeply antithetical to classical Hindu philosophy of tolerance for diversity. And multiple paths to salvation. So, in that deep sense, it is also 'anti-Hindu'.

STEPS BACKWARD

Freeing up Forest Land

In the name of easing business procedures, the requirement of a number of environmental clearances has been relaxed, and at times secretively. There have also been attempts to dilute the Forest Rights Act for the Adivasis that bypassed the mandatory concept of Adivasi Gram Sabhas in starting commercial operations on traditional forest lands.

Health Woes

There has been a retreat from the commitments by the UPA regime—and also the current regime in the early days—

on universal health coverage. Now, the announced National Health Policy of 2017 opens the doors for privatisation through its plans for 'strategic purchasing' of secondary and tertiary healthcare services, which is likely to hurt the availability and affordability of the services for the poor. In any case, India has one of the lowest percentages of GDP spent on health among the developing countries. Even though there have been promises made to increase it, so far we are nowhere there, and dismally so.

Cost of Vigilantism

The cow vigilantism and lynchings by the thugs belonging to or encouraged by the ruling party affiliates have had an economic effect, as it is playing havoc with livestock trade and transport. This has serious consequences for India's large livestock economy, and also for India's largest agricultural export—buffalo meat. Many people don't know that Gujarat is one of its major exporters.

Politics of Hate

In general, the increased incidents of hate crimes and social violence and the atmosphere of fear and intimidation for the minorities and the dissenters have caused serious damage to our social and political fabric. This, to me, is much more serious than any harm their bad policies may be causing to the economy.

The so-called Gujarat model of economic growth has so far not worked in large parts of the country, but the Gujarat model of hate and intolerance is very much in evidence everywhere. This is fostered by the Sangh *parivar* and its associates, aided and abetted by a conniving police and bureaucracy and encouraged by the selective silence of the Prime Minister.

It is selective silence interspersed with some 'wink-wink'

platitudes. He will talk about Dalits and Muslims and things like *'sabka saath'* and all that, but his party members know how to interpret his selective silence. In election rallies, in times of desperation, he is not averse to spewing some form of communal poison, as he did in Uttar Pradesh and Gujarat.

The government has failed to provide basic security for minorities and the minimum rule of law in this respect. The whole world now knows this and I am going to quote some global rankings. The government and the Prime Minister seem to be preoccupied with the World Bank's ease of doing business index. They do not seem to be aware that there are a lot of problems with this World Bank ranking, in which in any case India now ranks 100 instead of 130. Still quite bad. But one should give equal importance to some of the other rankings I am going to quote:

1. PEW Research Center brings out world ranking of 198 countries on religious tolerance. India is fourth from the bottom. That means India is one of the most intolerant countries in the whole world.
2. According to the World Press Freedom Index, brought out by media watchdog Reporters without Borders, India ranks 136 out of 180 countries.
3. The World Justice Project has a Rule of Law index and in it, India ranks 66 out of 113 countries, which is worse than Ghana, Jamaica, Senegal or Tunisia.

Danger for Democracy

In a sense, the current regime is presiding over a substantial deterioration in the quality of Indian democracy. This government is regularly imposing forms of obscurantism and intolerance on cultural institutions. They are packing the administrative bodies of educational institutions with bigots and charlatans. I should also add that the previous government also packed some of these bodies but there were fewer bigots and charlatans. And everybody knows that they are distorting history textbooks which schoolchildren read. This will be part of this regime's long-term social damage.

Finally, the erosion of fundamental institutions of the country, which began in the earlier regimes, has continued on an accelerated pace. That means abuse of police, bureaucracy, public investigating agencies and tax machinery for narrow and short-sighted purposes of political leaders. There is regular trampling of basic human rights of individuals in the name of sectarian communities taking offence or in the name of public order or national unity. This violates the letter and the spirit of our Constitution.

Meanwhile, the macroeconomic impasse with a mountain of bank loans and deceleration of private investments continues.

On the whole, the current regime's performance on the economy has been mediocre at best, but in socio-political matters, it has been far worse.

HOW MODI STACKS UP

Let's take 14 other points on governance.

1   **GST:**
    Started by the UPA. Pursued energetically by the NDA.
2   **AADHAAR:**
    Started by UPA. Pursued energetically by the NDA.
3   **FUEL SUBSIDY REDUCTION:**
    Started by the UPA; Pursued energetically by the NDA.
4   **MAKE IN INDIA:**
    NDA's big slogan is a continuation to the UPA's National Manufacturing Policy of 2011. So far, Make in India has delivered very little.
5   **SKILL INDIA:**
    Not delivered. The much-hyped but unattainable target of training at least 300 million by 2022 has been abandoned.
6   **SWACHH BHARAT:**
    An energetic continuation of the UPA regime's Nirmal Bharat campaign of building toilets, without considering

why many of these are not used. (This partly has to do with Hindu taboos of cleaning and emptying of pit latrines.)

7   PRADHAN MANTRI GRAM SADAK YOJANA:
Continuation to an earlier programme. Has worked reasonably well. In general, construction of highways and, in particular, rural roads have been quite successful.

8   ADMINISTRATIVE REFORMS:
Both Manmohan Singh and Narendra Modi had promised administrative reforms quite early in their tenure, but neither has delivered. On the contrary, Modi has centralised administration, which leads to bottlenecks, because all major decisions are taken in the PMO.

9   JAN DHAN:
Continuation to an earlier programme. No doubt, the Modi government's Jan Dhan programme is much more energetic. But many of these accounts are dormant or are duplicates.

10   BANKRUPTCY CODE:
This is a welcome step, but any significant change will depend on the judicial process.

11   CROP INSURANCE PROGRAMME:
The coverage has improved. So far, the use of technology in assessing crop damage and timely disbursement of claims have been too tardy.

12   UDAY:
The Ujwal DISCOM Assurance Yojana for takeover of the debts of power distribution companies is a step in the right direction but it is not a permanent solution. This is kind of a bailout. But we need to have a rationalisation of electricity tariff policy so that further bailouts will not be needed.

13   FOREIGN INVESTMENTS:
Much of the foreign investment is in the form of acquisitions and takeovers of existing ventures and buying of distressed assets of existing companies. These are not Greenfield investments. Some of it, in reality, may not

even be foreign but a form of recycling of Indian money through foreign tax havens.

14 TAMING INFLATION:

On paper, this claim is correct. It is hardly to the credit of the government as international prices declined. But it also had the misfortune because the first two years were drought years.

BASIC INCOME POLICY

The Safety Net of the Future

Indian Express, 28 December 2018

If social inequality is the most acutely felt social problem in India, insecurity, more than poverty, is the most acutely felt economic problem. While most measures suggest that only around one-fifth of the population today is under the official poverty line, large sections of them even much above that line are subject to brutal economic insecurities of various kinds (due to weather or health risks, market fluctuations, job uncertainties, etc). Anxiety about such insecurities occasionally spills over into the streets and politicians wake up and feel they have to do something.

In recent times both BJP (around election time in Uttar Pradesh and Maharashtra) and Congress (in Punjab, and now Rajasthan, Madhya Pradesh and Chhattisgarh) have rushed to the fire of farmer wrath with wild schemes of bank loan waivers. This is, of course, a bad idea not just because it plays havoc with the banking culture (just as that of loan waivers for corporate defaulters does), but most of it goes to help the middle and large farmers (more than two-thirds of our farmers are marginal farmers with less than 1 hectare of land, only 20% of whose loans are from banks, they owe the rest to private lenders, which the waiver programme will not touch).

Some politicians are now paying attention to the politically successful Rythu Bandhu example of income support to Telengana farmers (at about Rs 10,000 per hectare). The idea of income support is better than price support for farm products (which in any case does not help small farmers who mostly sell their produce to the traders at harvest time, and also applies in practice to a very limited number of crops and states). But it requires much better land records than we have in most states and leaves out the large numbers of even poorer landless workers.

All this distress arises directly or indirectly from India's singular failure in creating enough secure jobs. The farm distress is ultimately because of low productivity (due to lack of enough irrigation, cold storage and extension service, apart from the effects of climate change), and the low-earning farmers themselves want to move to non-farm jobs. This has been a failure of all political parties over many decades. The recent finger-pointing to the Prime Minister for the failure on the job front is only because he has been the loudest in promising jobs. The absence of secure jobs is also behind agitations on job reservations even by dominant castes (marathas, patidars, jats, kapus, etc) and behind the mobilisation of lumpen elements of the ruling party affiliates in various incidents of extortion in the name of cow protection and minority lynchings.

To put our mind to the difficult task of creating a sufficient number of secure jobs is, of course, highly imperative. But it is a long-term project (with some exceptions like the important proposal for extending the employment guarantee scheme to urban-sector public works as well). Meanwhile, extending schemes of social protection for relief of the massive economic insecurity is urgent and politically expedient.

One idea is that of a Universal Basic Income Supplement (UBIS), which avoids some of the problems that we have mentioned for loan waivers and farm income support per hectare, and also some of the administrative and incentive problems of most insurance schemes (the much-hyped current farm insurance premium subsidy scheme has been hobbled by low participation and tardy claim settlements, often benefiting private insurance companies more than the farmers). UBIS should be looked upon not as an anti-poverty programme, but mainly as part of the citizens' right to minimum economic security.

BUT WHAT ABOUT THE FISCAL COST OF UBIS?

We know that the highly defective loan waiver programme, if applied to all states in India, will easily cost more than 4 trillion rupees. The farm income support plan at the Telangana rate for all of India will also come to more than half of that amount.

The feasibility of a UBIS, of course, depends on the size of the supplement one has in mind, and mainly on the political will to increase the tax-GDP ratio, and (assuming that none of the existing major anti-poverty programmes will be significantly scaled down) to cut down on various subsidies largely enjoyed by the better-off sections of the population. It has been estimated that the latter subsidies (for the central and state governments together) currently come to about 6% of GDP; another 6% of GDP is in the form of 'revenues foregone' or tax concessions in the central budget—take at most one-third of this (2%), since some of these concessions may be helping necessary business; think of another 2% of GDP from taxing currently exempted wealth, inheritance and long-term capital gains, and currently under-assessed and under-taxed property values in urban and peri-urban areas (at a time when the National Sample Survey evidence suggests that our wealth inequality is mounting, and is already in the Latin American range). All this adds to a mobilisable surplus of about 10% of GDP.

There are important and legitimate claims on these resources for programmes of infrastructure building, health and education. But at least a quarter of these resources can pay for a decent UBIS for everybody (a household of 5 people can get about 16,000 rupees per year). To start with, give it only to women, which will halve the cost; on a rough estimate it will then cost about 2.1 trillion rupees or about 1.25% of the current GDP.

The fiscal bureaucrats, of course, will shake their heads and consider all this unrealistic. But we should let the politicians know that the potential is there to tax (and reduce the subsidies for) the better-off and address India's staggering problem of economic insecurity. If we fail to do that, it is a political failure for which we have to pay dearly (both in terms of economic welfare and our democracy) in near enough future.

Guaranteed Minimum Income

Bloomberg Quint, 30 January 2019

The Congress Party has reportedly announced a guaranteed minimum income for every poor person in India along with a national loan waiver scheme for farmers. The waiver is a singularly bad idea, whether for loans to farmers or to corporate magnates. But the former is an idea worth discussing.

In March 2011, in an article in the *Economic & Political Weekly*, I had recommended a Universal Basic Income (UBI) for India (pp.7-10), funded by withdrawing the government subsidies that currently go mainly to the better-off sections of the population. This is different from what the Congress Party has now proposed, partly because my idea applied to everybody not just the poor, and partly because without a proper scheme of funding it is difficult to judge the worthwhileness of a proposal.

One problem of confining the guaranteed income only to the poor is that in India finding the real poor has always been a tricky administrative issue, riddled with malfeasance. All-India survey data show that about one-half of those who are below the official Indian poverty line do not have the BPL (below the poverty line) card, while about one third of the non-poor have the card.

Also, I look upon UBI not mainly as an anti-poverty programme, but more as part of a citizen's right to minimum economic security (under the Supreme Court's broad interpretation of the 'right to life'). This minimum economic security is important not just for those below the poverty line. Large numbers of people above the poverty line suffer from all kinds of brutal economic insecurities (vagaries of weather affecting crops, market fluctuations, health risks, job uncertainties and so on). A UBI can provide some minimum insurance against such risks, without the usual incentive and verification problems of commercial insurance. Most advanced countries have social security for workers, but the overwhelming majority of workers in India are informal, and are thus mainly unprotected from those economic insecurities. Also, the overwhelming majority of adult women in India do not have any outside income, so a UBI regularly deposited in their bank account can go a long way in raising their currently low status and autonomy within the family.

In recent months, there has been some discussion about the farm income support programmes implemented in Telengana and announced in Odisha. The Telengana programme is for income support per acre, and hence highly regressive, as larger farmers get more. Also, land records in most states in India are much worse than in Telengana, making fair implementation very difficult. The Odisha programme is not per acre but per farmer, but the latter in reality can be a very slippery category in administrative identification. A UBI programme does not require such identification. It will, of course, require a bank account or access to a banking agent. Such access will improve with UBI as the fixed costs of operations of a banking agent get spread out over larger numbers. So a UBI programme should be really universal, not for only the poor or the farmers, or even only for the rural sector—the latter, apart from some identification problems, may be unfair to the millions of urban poor and other insecure people. Even though conceptually I look upon UBI as a part of the right to minimum economic security for all, I'd not strenuously object if there are unambiguously clean ways of excluding the very rich.

The crucial issue, which most political party proposals evade, is that of funding any UBI programme. In my writings, I have suggested three sources: (a) withdrawing the subsidies that are mostly enjoyed by the rich and middle classes—the estimate for them for 2015-16 comes to about 6% of GDP; (b) taking about one-third (i.e. 2% of GDP) of what is labelled as 'revenues foregone' in central budgets mainly in the form of tax concessions to business which in all come to another 6% of GDP; and (c) raising more taxes on the rich amounting to say another 2% of GDP—levying taxes on currently exempt wealth and inheritance of wealth and high agricultural incomes, and raising more taxes from currently under-taxed long-term capital gains and land and property values in urban and peri-urban areas. These three sources add up to 10% of GDP as mobilisable surplus.

Of course, there are other legitimate claims on this surplus, like more expenditure on health, education and infrastructure. Taking that into account, if even one quarter of the surplus can be spent on UBI, at current prices, this will allow a UBI for about Rs 18,000 per household. It is important to note that this does not touch any of the current welfare programmes. If a UBI is announced that substantially impairs the current budget for essential programmes like the rural employment guarantee scheme, mid-day meals in schools or child nutrition programmes like ICDS, I'll vigorously oppose such a UBI.

This does not, of course, mean that the current welfare programmes do not need to shed some waste and inefficiency. It is also possible that some of the more than 900 centrally sponsored schemes are ripe for rationalisation and pruning; if some funds are saved on that account, they may add to the above-mentioned mobilisable surplus. I can also see that for some welfare programmes better governance may be more important than more money. For example in 9 of the poorest states, covering nearly half of the total population, much of even the paltry budget on health allocated to them goes unspent each year.

It is often claimed in some elite quarters that UBI will make people idle or induce them to spend more on alcohol and drugs. Careful experimental data in different developing countries (including India) do not show any evidence of this. The lazy poor is an old canard the rich have used over centuries. The poor in India are often overworked, particularly the women, and I want a world in which they have to slog a little less.

In general, in a country where politicians are prone to give patronage in the form of handouts and job reservations to client groups, I'd prefer a world where redistributive and welfare programmes are genuinely universal (like UBI or universal health care or universal access to vocational training), proudly claimed as part of citizens' minimum rights, rather than bestowed on particular client groups who come to politicians as supplicants.

I also have no illusion that the Indian rich will easily give up on the subsidies and low taxes they have enjoyed. If UBI has to be funded from that source, labour organisations (both in the formal and informal sectors) and civil society groups have to make such programmes salient parts of their agenda and actively lobby and agitate for them.

Basic Income
for a Poor Country

Ideas for India, 26 September 2016

The (by now old) idea of recasting the Welfare State by giving everyone—rich or poor—an unconditional basic income seems to have begun to catch the public imagination both on the left and the right. The left regards it as a simple and potentially comprehensive antidote to poverty; the right finds in it a way to demolish the complex welfare bureaucracy and yet to meet some social transfer obligations without harming incentives much. It also provides an assurance for the dreaded future when robots may replace many of us in the workplace. Even though on 5 June 2016 Swiss voters rejected the idea in a referendum, Canada, Holland, and Finland are reported to be actively flirting with it.

In the US and the UK, some prominent economists have dismissed the idea as simply unaffordable. In the US, for example, a handout of US $ 10,000 to everyone—which is less than the existing official poverty threshold for a single person—has been estimated to exhaust almost all of the tax revenue collected by the federal government today. So the fiscal arithmetic does not seem to make sense.

But does it make sense for a poor to medium-income country? It turns out, surprisingly, that it may very well be feasible there, apart from being desirable. This is partly because the poverty threshold is low, and because the existing social safety nets are often threadbare and costly to administer.

Take the case of India. The official poverty line is very low and yet about one-fifth of the population lives below it. Under the current anti-poverty programmes, you are eligible for relief if you hold a BPL (below-poverty-line) card. Yet surveys, for example, the recent one by India Human Development Survey (IHDS) show that about half of the Indian poor do not have the card and about one-third of the non-poor have it. In many programmes targeted at the poor, through a process of political and administrative collusion and connivance, benefits continue to leak out to non-targeted better-off people, while many of the intended beneficiaries are left out. In a country where the large majority of workers are in the informal sector, often self-employed, without benefits and without account-keeping or any income data, means-testing is often impossible. In general, the process of identifying the poor by some official criterion is costly, corrupt, complicated and controversial. An unconditional and Universal Basic Income (UBI) can cut through much of this mess.

FISCAL FEASIBILITY

But how is one going to pay for it? Will it involve a large increase in the burden for taxpayers? Not necessarily. Let us show some back-of-the-envelope calculations for India.

Suppose we decide to fix the unconditional basic income at an inflation-indexed Rs 10,000 at 2014-15 prices (this is about three-quarters of the official poverty line that year) to be paid to each person per year in India's the-then population of 1.25 billion. (At the moment, to keep calculations simple, I am ignoring the adult-child difference in needs; besides, once you introduce this difference, an official gets to have power over eligibility of families to the total amounts, as many do not have birth certificates to indicate age.) This comes to about 10% of the Indian GDP (Gross Domestic Product) that year. We know from past estimates (these estimates are now being updated) of economists associated with the National Institute of Public Finance and Policy (NIPFP) in Delhi that every year the Indian government gives out about 14% of GDP in (implicit or explicit) subsidies for the central and state governments together. Roughly about two-thirds of these subsidies are described as 'non-merit', that is mostly going to the better-off sections of the population; so that amounts to about 9% of GDP. This deliberately excludes subsidies for health, education, nutrition, environment, rural and urban development programmes, etc (so the significant leakages from these programmes to the non-target better-off groups are not included in the above-mentioned 9%). Similarly, all of food subsidies are included in the list of 'merit' subsidies, even though it is arguable that subsidies in the form of support prices for agricultural products largely go to richer farmers, just as it is arguable that subsidies to higher education largely go to the better-off sections.

On top of the 9% of GDP in the form of regressive subsidies there is a category of 'revenues foregone' in the Central Budget (mostly in the form of tax holidays and exemptions) largely for firms or companies—this comes to about 6% of GDP (no one has yet estimated the revenues foregone in the state budgets). There are data and interpretation problems for the tax exemption figures; there are grounds to believe that they are overestimates of the potential revenue source, as they, for example, include necessary exemptions from customs duty for imports used in processing for re-exports. Yet if even half of the 6% is added to the earlier 9% for the regressive subsidies, the total easily exceeds the 10% of GDP required for the Rs 10,000 per person basic income. So, if the government so wants, it can pay out that proposed basic income to everyone, rich or poor, without any fresh taxation, if only the subsidies and tax exemptions to the better-off are discontinued.

If the government does not have the political courage to discontinue them to the full extent, to that extent one will, of course, need either some more taxes (for example, by carrying out some simple reforms on the administrative process of the absurdly low-value assessments and property tax collections in India where the real estate sector has been booming off and on for many years) or a lower basic income payout. In any case, a reasonable minimum basic income is very much within the realm of fiscal feasibility. With the biometric identification programme Aadhaar and the bank account programme Jan Dhan soon reaching the overwhelming majority of the people, the administrative feasibility problem for a universal grant should be smoothened out over time. It should be administered by the central government (with the Finance Commission making appropriate adjustments to the fiscal transfers to the states, if part of its funding is to come from state subsidies).

DESIRABILITY

Let us now comment a bit on its desirability. The basic income scheme, while it can replace some egregiously dysfunctional current welfare policies, should not be thought of as a substitute for some other key welfare policies (like public education and healthcare or pre-school child nutrition programmes or the employment guarantee programme on public works). This is important because even with cash in hand the poor, for example, may not by themselves spend on health or child nutrition to the socially desirable extent.

European social democrats sometimes resist the basic income proposal, even when it is not to replace some existing welfare policies, because any weakening of their current social insurance programmes may undermine the worker solidarity in which they originated, or because they weigh the social value of work beyond the income it generates (whereas basic income is not conditional on any work for society), or they worry about the morale problem in a society divided into diligent workers and indolent grant-receivers.

I think these arguments are less forceful for poor countries.

In any case, most poor countries do not currently have social insurance for the overwhelming majority of the people who are in the large informal sector.

And as for the dignity and solidarity-enhancing value of work, any feasible basic income for countries like India in the foreseeable future will be so small that it will not significantly replace work. If anything the poor are often overworked in back-breaking oppressive work, and it will be better if they, particularly women, can work a little less. In particular, it can be a great relief for the stark livelihood uncertainties faced daily by the vast numbers of the self-employed and the marginalised casual and migrant workers, and will help them in seeking better jobs. It will also enhance their bargaining power against the traders, middlemen, contractors, creditors and landlords they encounter. For women, it can boost their autonomy within the household, and for the self-employed poor like small producers and vendors, it can relieve a part of their credit constraint. For the socially stigmatised workers in India, like scavengers and waste-carriers, basic income can provide an escape ladder, and induce society to mechanise as much as possible such unwanted filthy jobs.

A possible economic argument against giving out cash as opposed to goods and services in kind is that in remote places the supply of essential goods may not be there unless publicly provided, or more generally, monopoly suppliers may hike the prices to neutralise the extra income. The counter-argument to this is that even in remote places, over time, demand is likely to generate its own supply, and the goods the poor consume are often labour-intensive goods where the barriers to entry for firms are not large, so monopolies may be easy to break.

A more common argument against basic income in poor countries is that the poor (particularly the men in the household) will blow it up on alcohol, drugs and gambling. One can, of course, try to deposit the basic income for the household in the adult woman's bank account. But more importantly, there is actually not much evidence of misuse of the grant in the accumulating experimental evidence on this. There are now many experiments in different parts of the world on the use of unconditional cash grants, where most of the money is found to be spent on worthwhile goods and services. (Keeping in mind the few able-bodied but feckless people who may misuse the grant, the employment guarantee programme on public works is retained in our list as a fallback option.)

Thus even if the currently-discussed basic income proposal turns out to be only a gleam in the eye of utopian socialists and libertarians, the scare stories of its expensiveness in rich countries should not deter trying it out in poor to middle-income countries. The low poverty threshold and the inequality in the current distribution of government subsidies in the latter countries provide an opportunity which makes such a proposal remarkably affordable, apart from its being relatively easy on the scarce administrative resources of such governments.

POLITICAL FEASIBILITY

Finally, how politically feasible is this proposal for countries like India? It is a long shot but worth trying. Many people who otherwise like the idea throw up their hands and say that the better-off in India will never give up the subsidies they enjoy (which incidentally come to several times our total anti-poverty budgets). My own position is that instead of reconciling ourselves to the massive dole we give every year to the rich, we should think in terms of mobilising public opinion and activate social movements on a platform like UBI which otherwise some people both on the left and the right find acceptable. The way to start is first to convince all the informal workers' associations and welfare boards in India about the feasibility and desirability of basic income, as they will be the largest beneficiaries. Then these associations—maybe SEWA (Self-Employed Women's Association), which already supports the basic income idea—can take the leadership in this and negotiate with the organised-sector worker unions about how basic income is really an extension of the idea of pension, but for everybody. What do the trade unions gain from this negotiation? One, they get a much larger body of workers to be associated in their demands and bargains. Basic income can be a common bridge between the unionised and the vastly larger number of other workers, a divide which for many years has weakened the labour movement. Second, today one-third to 40% of workers in the organised sector are contract labourers deprived of most benefits. Unions have been demanding benefits for the latter for some time; their struggle will be strengthened if it now becomes part of a much larger movement.

Even if the workers, both formal and informal, get united on this, the strength of the opposition from business, rich farmers and the salaried class should not be underestimated, as in my scheme the latter groups will have to give up some of the subsidies they currently enjoy. Will rich farmers, for example, give up on minimum support prices and subsidies for fertiliser, water and electricity in exchange of each family (say, of five people) getting Rs 50,000 as basic income? At least, they may now have some difficulties in mobilising small farmers for their cause. (One reason I have kept the figure of basic income at a relatively high figure—amounting to 10% of GDP—is that a higher figure may encourage small farmers and other such people to rally behind it instead of the trickle-down subsidies they currently get that are mainly lapped up by the richer people.) No doubt, the whole process will involve tough negotiations and give-and-take all through. At least, one argument the rich usually give against welfare schemes for the poor that much of it is stolen or wasted will apply much less in the case of basic income.

One should have no illusion about the difficulties in the political-economy process for implementing basic income. But one thing going in its favour is that it attracts support from people in different parts of the political spectrum, which may someday generate a winning coalition.

This is a revised and enlarged version of an article that came out in Project Syndicate on 22 June 2016. The author's first exposition of the basic income idea in the Indian context was published in Economic & Political Weekly, 5 March 2011 (pp.3-17).

REFERENCES

Porter, E, 'A Universal Basic Income Is a Poor Tool to Fight Poverty', *New York Times,* 31 May 2016

Self-Employed Women's Association (SEWA) Bharat, 'A Little More, How Much It Is...Piloting Basic Income Transfers in Madhya Pradesh, India', UNICEF India, 2014

Srivastava, D K, C B Rao, P Chakraborty & T S Rangamannar, 'Budgetary Subsidies in India. Subsidising Social and Economic Services', National Institute of Public Finance and Policy (NIPFP), 2003

The Politics of UBI

Times of India, 3 May 2017

The old idea of Universal Basic Income (UBI)—of the state paying everybody a uniform amount as part of welfare—is getting some traction in political discourse worldwide. On the left, it is regarded as a simple antidote to poverty. On the right, it is viewed as a means to demolish complex welfare bureaucracies while meeting some social transfer obligations without weakening work incentives significantly.

In India, apart from its anti-poverty potential, it can also be a substantial measure to improve autonomy (say, of adult women, three-quarters of whom do not earn income) and dignity by giving workers an escape ladder from socially despised occupations (scavenging, waste-carrying, prostitution, etc).

I have heard people, otherwise favourably disposed to the idea of UBI, opposing it primarily for reasons of ultimately political expediency. Some fiscal bureaucrats/economists say that we cannot afford it as it'll simply be an add-on to the fiscal burden since the vested interests against replacing existing welfare programmes are too strong. Another group, mainly social activists, come from the opposite end: they say talking of UBI is a ploy to politically undermine some of the existing welfare programmes which are working reasonably well. I have some disagreement with both groups.

Let me first clarify some issues of the fiscal space which both groups raise. The most recent estimates (made at the National Institute of Public Finance and Policy) suggest that (central plus state) subsidies that mainly go to better-off people ('non-merit subsidies') amount to about 5% of GDP. In addition, the central budget alone shows 'revenues foregone' (primarily tax concessions to companies) coming to about 6% of GDP. Even if one-third of these revenues foregone are made available for this purpose, added to the non-merit subsidies, it comes to 7% of GDP potentially available for UBI, which is a substantial sum, more than twice the total amount currently spent on all anti-poverty programmes.

Moreover, there is no reason why we should assume there is no scope for more taxation. The tax-GDP ratio in India is substantially lower than in China, Brazil and some other developing countries. Our real estate and property tax assessments are absurdly low compared to their market value. We have zero taxation of agricultural income, long-term capital gains in equity markets, and of wealth and inheritance —this is at a time when our wealth inequality is mounting (even from NSS household survey data which underestimate the wealth of the rich, the standard Gini coefficient measure of asset inequality rose from 0.66 in 1991-92 to 0.75 in 2011-12, which is now in the Latin American range).

So if India can divert some of the subsidies (and revenues foregone) from their current better-off recipients and introduce significant fresh taxation of the rich, UBI of about a thousand rupees per person per month is fiscally affordable. I'd not object if with a smaller UBI, parts of the extra revenues are spent on public goods like health, education and infrastructure.

Some resources may also be released by terminating some of the particularly wasteful welfare programmes, but I am against UBI replacing current programmes like ICDS, mid-day meals, and NREGA. As an experiment, UBI may begin only with women, maybe in urban areas until banking services spread to remote areas and in states where current welfare measures are particularly leaky.

I am often asked, do you want to pay this money even to the rich? Yes, primarily because normatively I want UBI as part of a basic right of every citizen to minimum economic security. (Practically, if some asset threshold can be transparently implemented to exclude the very rich, I'll not object. The history of targeting in India is, unfortunately, riddled with controversy and corruption.) To the extent UBI is funded by taxes and withheld current subsidies to the rich, the money otherwise is already going to the rich. Also, part of UBI to the rich will return to the government in the form of taxes.

For far too long the default redistributive option for Indian politicians has been job reservation and subsidisation of private goods (food, fertilisers, fuel, credit, etc). I want bureaucratic and political attention to be focussed more on public goods and welfare services that are universal—like UBI, universal healthcare, etc—away from the structures of patronage distribution to particular groups or individuals.

Of course, the better-off in India—businessmen, rich farmers, the salaried class—will not easily give up on the subsidies and handouts they currently enjoy. This means we should think in terms of mobilising public opinion and activate social movements on a platform like UBI. In particular, as the workers in the informal sector will be the largest beneficiaries of UBI, it can provide a common bridge between them and the unionised formal sector workers, a divide which for many years has weakened the labour movement. Today about one-third of workers even in the organised sector are contract labourers deprived of most benefits. Unions have been demanding benefits for the latter for some time; their struggle will be strengthened if it now becomes part of a much larger movement for UBI.

One should have no illusion about the difficulties in the political process for implementing UBI. But one thing going in its favour is that it attracts support from people in different parts of the political spectrum, which may someday generate a winning coalition.

Universal Basic Income—
Its Special Case for India

Indian Journal of Human Development,
11 January 2018

The idea of universal unconditional grant to all is an old idea in western countries. It has been associated with Thomas More (1516); Thomas Paine (1797); in the 19th century, Charles Fourier, the French 'utopian' socialist, and John Stuart Mill inspired by him; in the 20th, Bertrand Russell, Rev Martin Luther King Jr, three Nobel Laureate economists—Friedrich Hayek, James Meade, Jim Tobin (the latter in connection with the McGovern presidential campaign of 1972, which included a promise of a 'demogrant'), various Green Parties in Europe, and so on.

It has been often opposed by those who think the work disincentives (from income effect, though there is no substitution effect) may undermine the prevailing social contract.

Some voters also dislike the idea of giving public money to the rich as well.

Also, by the current standards, it may be too expensive for rich countries. For example, a $10,000 basic income for each citizen in the US (somewhat below the US poverty line) will exhaust the budget.

But now there are some new adherents in the West in view of the looming 'take over' of the workplace by AI and robots.

In India, I do not take the work disincentive argument very seriously. Poor workers are, if anything, overworked, particularly women.

Also, poverty lines are so low, and regressive subsidies so large that a significant UBI may be potentially feasible.

There are four special reasons for UBI in India:

- Targeting the poor is so complicated, corrupt and controversial. Just to give an example from the case of BPL (below the poverty line) card, which is indispensable for many of the targeted welfare programmes in India. The India Human Development Survey data for all-India in 2011-12 indicate that about half of the poor do not have the card, while one-third of the non-poor have it.
- In a country where the politics of redistribution is often centred around group-specific or individual-specific patronage—like job reservation, and subsidised private goods (food, fuel, fertilisers, credit, etc), the argument in favour of universality—UBI, universal health care, universal pensions, etc—has a special appeal, particularly if normatively one thinks of them as part of minimum citizenship rights, rather than clientelistic favours dispensed by politicians.
- In a country where when three-quarters of adult women do not earn any income, UBI can boost autonomy of women within the family.
- It can also be an escape ladder for people in stigmatised occupations in Indian society (manual scavenging, animal skinning, prostitution, etc).

The idea of UBI often faces three kinds of opposition:
(a) opposition from fiscal bureaucrats, as it may break the budget;
(b) opposition from social activists who regard this as a ploy

to undermine existing welfare programmes, which are
working reasonably well;
(c) opposition from both groups that any extra money should
better be spent on education, health and infrastructure.

First a few points on the fiscal arithmetic:

• Mundle and Sikdar have estimated that of the total
subsidies of the central and state governments (both
explicit and implicit) in 2011-12 what can be considered
as 'non-merit' subsidies—i.e. mainly going to the better-
off sections of the population—come to about 5% of GDP.

• In the central budget alone what are called Revenues
Foregone (mainly tax concessions to companies) come to
more than 6%. Some of these concessions may be essential
(for example, in the case of customs duty exemptions for
re-exports), but it is not too unreasonable to take one-
third of the total (i.e. 2% of GDP) as potentially available.
This does not count the Revenues Foregone in state
government budgets, for which we do not have good
estimates.

• There is also considerable scope for fresh taxes. The tax-
GDP ratio in India is substantially lower than in China,
Brazil and some other developing countries. Our real
estate and property tax assessments are absurdly low
compared to their market value. We have zero taxation
of agricultural income, of long-term capital gains in equity
markets, and of wealth and inheritance. This is at a time
when our wealth inequality is mounting—even from NSS
household survey data which underestimate the wealth
of the rich, the standard Gini coefficient measure of asset
inequality rose from 0.66 in 1991-92 to 0.75 in 2011-12,
which is now in the Latin American range.

All combined, there is a potential for mobilising about 10%
of GDP, allowing for a significant UBI *plus* extra expenditure
on health, education, and infrastructure, and no replacement

of existing welfare programmes (if some wasteful ones among them are replaced, the potential can exceed 10% of GDP).

On health and education governance issues are even more serious than the paucity of funds that are officially allocated to them. On health, for example, it has been reported that in the nine poorest states of India (accounting for nearly half of India's total population) even the paltry amounts budgeted for health goes substantially unspent by the end of the fiscal year. So just throwing more money into these accounts will not solve some of the recalcitrant problems.

I am against replacement of some major welfare programmes like ICDS, mid-day meals, NREGA, etc. Their economic rationale is independent of that for UBI. So I'll be against UBI if it is to replace programmes like these. My search for alternative sources of funding is primarily motivated by my objective of NOT replacing them.

In any case, I think the discussion of UBI is at such an early stage that it should be conducted at two levels of abstraction— one is at the conceptual level of its acceptability in the Indian context, and the other at a more concrete level of the exigencies of its implementation. In this paper, I do not discuss very much at the latter level—for example, I am not suggesting any particular rate of payment under UBI. Even though I have shown that about 10% of GDP is potentially mobilisable, if the social consensus is in favour of spending somewhat more in effective investment for health, education or infrastructure, and somewhat less for UBI, I'll not seriously object.

I should note, however, that one argument for a relatively large UBI is that it may then succeed in weaning some of the small farmers and workers away from allying with the much richer beneficiaries of the current regressive subsidies.

Similarly, I am not here addressing secondary-level questions like if UBI should be indexed or not—my inclination is to suggest indexation, just as we do in a way for salary and pensions in the formal sector. Similarly, at the implementation stage, depending on the mobilisation of financial and organisational resources in different states, one can start with some experiments with UBI at a pilot level.

For example, one may try it out on an experimental basis:

(a) Only for women
(b) Only in some states where the requisite fiscal, banking, and political capacity exist
(c) Maybe first only in urban areas, where the informational and banking constraints may be less acute

At the general conceptual level I am often asked, do you want to pay this money even to the rich like the Ambanis? My answer is yes, primarily because normatively I want UBI as part of a basic right of every citizen to minimum economic security. Just as we recognise the right of Ambanis for police protection against crime as a basic right for them, even though they can very much afford their own private protection services, we should not deny them the right to a basic income. (Practically, if some asset threshold—car ownership, a threshold in income tax return, etc—can be transparently implemented to exclude the very rich, I'll not object.) To the extent, UBI is funded by taxes and withheld current subsidies to the rich, one should keep in mind that even without UBI the money otherwise is already going to the rich. Also, part of UBI paid to the rich will return to the government in the form of taxes.

I also want to emphasise the conceptual point that the idea of UBI is primarily for minimum economic security for all citizens. Poverty eradication is not the main goal. So I find some of the discussion on how good an anti-poverty measure UBI is somewhat irrelevant for the present purpose. Large numbers of people, even those above the poverty line, suffer from brutal insecurities of different kinds (arising from weather risks, market risks, health risks, etc), and a floor basic income is part insurance against such risks, without the administrative costs of checking for the usual problems of moral hazard and adverse selection that commercial insurance projects involve.

If we are thinking of funding UBI from regressive subsidies, of course, the better-off in India—businessmen, rich farmers, the salaried class—will not easily give up on the subsidies and handouts they currently enjoy. This means we should think in terms of mobilising public opinion and activate social movements on a platform like UBI. In particular, as the workers in the informal sector will be the largest beneficiaries of UBI, it can provide a common bridge between them and the unionised formal sector workers, a divide which for many years has weakened the labour movement. Today about one-third of workers even in the organised sector are contract labourers deprived of most benefits. Unions have been demanding benefits for the latter for some time; their struggle will be strengthened if it now becomes part of a much larger movement for UBI.

One should have no illusion about the difficulties in the political process for implementing UBI. But one thing going in its favour is that it attracts support from people in different parts of the political spectrum, which may someday generate a winning coalition.

Funding of Universal Basic Income

Indian Express, 16 January 2019

After my last op-ed in this paper ('The Safety Net of the Future', 28 December 2018; pp.120-124) several readers, intrigued by the idea of a Universal Basic Income Supplement (UBIS) proposed in the article, asked me to elaborate. Hence this article.

There are reports that the ruling party in Sikkim has announced UBIS in its election manifesto, and, more intriguingly, the Centre is considering such a measure 'for people below the Poverty Line'. The latter is a contradiction in terms: UBIS is an unconditional grant to all citizens, not just to the poor—that's what 'universal' means. As I wrote in my earlier piece, many people, who are much above the official poverty line, suffer from variety of insecurities—farmers, of course, face weather and market risks but non-farmers also face several kinds of risks, including in their jobs, often in the informal sector, where some of them are refugees from agrarian and ecological distress or are victims of the recent disaster of demonetisation.

UBIS avoids the problem of deciphering who is poor and who is not, which is an intricate problem in India—the India Human Development Survey found that in 2011-12 about half of the officially poor did not have the BPL card, while about one-third of the non-poor had it. In any case, I look upon UBIS not as an administratively easier anti-poverty programme; to me, it is more a part of a citizen's right to minimum economic security, a right which many countries recognise, but so far India does not, even though it should easily fall under the Supreme Court's interpretation of the 'right to life' in the Constitution.

I am often asked: Do you want the government to give money to the Ambanis as well? My answer is yes, as citizens they are entitled to it, just as they have the right to get police protection, even though they can afford their own protection. (If in practice some rich people do not claim it or if there are transparent ways of excluding them—for example those above a certain threshold in income tax return or owning cars, etc— I will not object strenuously, even though the conceptual point of a citizen's right remains.)

Since UBIS is to be given to the rich and the middle classes as well, it can be expensive. In my earlier piece, I suggested funding it from reducing some of the subsidies that are at present enjoyed mainly by the better-off, also taking a bit from the various tax concessions mostly to business (called 'revenues foregone' in the Central Budget), and taxing the currently exempt wealth, inheritance, and long-term capital gains, and collecting more taxes from the currently under-assessed and under-taxed property values. Only a quarter of the 10 per cent of GDP thus potentially mobilisable could go to UBIS; the rest can be spent on infrastructure, health and education. This allows roughly a grant of about Rs 16,000 to each household. If, to start with, it is given only to women, it'll halve the cost. The special treatment to women is recognition of the hard work most of them do for their households, and outside. It is also a means to raise their (currently low) autonomy and status within the Indian family.

Of course, the better-off (businessmen, large farmers, the salaried class) will not easily give up on the subsidies they have enjoyed all these years or pay substantially more taxes.

But without that, if UBIS merely adds significantly to the fiscal deficit or is funded by scaling down some of the current major anti-poverty programmes, then I'll be generally against it. It will only show that the policy-makers are politically afraid to touch the rich. (This does not mean that the current anti-poverty programmes do not need to shed their waste and inefficiencies.)

I think packaging a significant UBIS with a simultaneous increase in the taxes on the rich will help macro-economic stability, apart from assuaging the poor who will face some of the price rise in commodities or services, when subsidies are withdrawn (for example, the price of urea will rise for all farmers, if the fertiliser subsidy is curtailed, even though most of the subsidy goes to large farmers and factories). It is also important to keep in mind that if the declared UBIS amount is too small, only serving as a rhetorical token before elections, people will see through it as another electoral 'jumla', too many of which have been associated with the current regime.

Then there are some practicalities of UBIS any policy-maker has to consider. One, how do you reach everybody in India when many people still do not have bank accounts or access to banking agents (although once such a programme starts, banking agents are likely to be induced to expand their operations, as fixed costs are spread out over larger numbers)? Two, Aadhaar or some other form of identification will be necessary, but the horror stories one has heard about the poor being denied PDS because of the lack of Aadhaar authentication make one wary of bureaucratic callousness in this respect. Three, UBIS needs to be transparently linked right from the beginning to some cost of living index—this is particularly important because of the callous way Indian governments have let their contribution under the National Old Age Pensions Scheme stagnate at a measly Rs 200 per month per pensioner for the last 12 years. Four, UBIS could be different for adults and children, but one probably should not go that way because in the absence of proper age records it may give an opportunity to some corrupt officials. Five, how should the grant money be allocated between the Centre and the states? The state governments have to be part of the active negotiations. Different states may have different fiscal capacities and also different kinds of logistical capabilities in reaching out to people, particularly in remote areas. In the estimate for subsidies to the better-off (referred to in my earlier piece), state-level subsidies have been included. In the beginning, however, the central government may have to bear most of the cost, and the Finance Commission may have to work out the eventual modalities of allocation of the burden between the Centre and the states.

UBIS is a policy issue that requires our serious attention and deliberation. It is not one for politicians in desperation for something to do for angry voters just before elections.

On Piketty's Arguments against Basic Income: How Applicable are they to India?

The Wire, 17 December 2016

The Wire recently carried a translated version of an op-ed piece that my long-time friend Thomas Piketty wrote for *Le Monde* on 13 December 2016, arguing against the idea of basic income for France. Since some of us have argued in favour of a Universal Basic Income (UBI) for India—see, for example, the symposium in the blog 'Ideas for India' in September 2016—it is important to point out that Piketty's arguments do not necessarily negate the arguments for UBI in India.

Piketty thinks France should aim higher than just a basic income of 530 or 800 Euros per month, 'to formulate more ambitious objectives which cover the distribution of income and wealth in its entirety and, consequently, the distribution of access to power and opportunities'. To those of us who are egalitarians, such lofty objectives are admirable as long-term goals also for India, but under the existing political constraints, if we can achieve UBI at a reasonable minimum level, it'll be a big step forward. I doubt if Piketty would want the best to be the enemy of the good.

Piketty advocates steeply progressive income and wealth taxes, but in India only about 1% of people actually pay any income tax, and the wealth and inheritance taxes have been abolished, the former recently and the latter three decades back. India used to have steeply progressive income taxes with very high marginal rates, but they often led to large-scale tax evasion. While there is some scope for more progressive taxes in India, particularly on capital gains and real estate and agriculture, we have to think of other available means of redistribution. Similarly, Piketty advocates a 'fair wage', but we have to keep in mind that in our country even the statutory paltry minimum wage is not earned by the vast majority of workers who are in the informal sector.

Since the supporters of UBI do not want it in any way to substitute for attempts to improve education and health, we should whole-heartedly endorse Piketty's call for more egalitarian education policies. Similarly, we should also support his call for more worker participation in governance within the firm, as in Germany and Sweden, an issue to which our trade unions have not paid enough attention. These principles of social welfare and better governance are in no way contradictory to UBI in India.

There are also special circumstances in favour of UBI in India that may not apply to Europe:

- First, in India, the process of identifying the poor for programmes targeted to them is often costly, corrupt, complicated and controversial—survey data, for example, suggests that for India as a whole, half of the poor do not have the BPL (below the poverty line) card while one-third of the non-poor have it. Since UBI does not have to identify the poor, it is administratively much easier and cleaner.
- Secondly, for women of both poor and middle-class households, a regular deposit of a basic income in their bank accounts can give a hefty boost to their autonomy within the family. Similarly, for the socially stigmatised workers in India, like scavengers and waste-carriers, UBI can provide an escape ladder and induce society to mechanise as much as possible such unwanted filthy jobs.

- Thirdly, for the vast masses of the self-employed poor and the marginalised casual and migrant workers (without access to any of the welfare benefits that Piketty's compatriot French workers currently enjoy), UBI can be a great relief for the stark livelihood uncertainties they face daily. It will also enhance their bargaining power against the traders, middlemen, contractors, creditors and landlords they encounter.

In my piece in the Ideas for India symposium, I have suggested that a UBI of Rs 10,000 per person is financially feasible if it is funded by the total subsidies that, according to some estimates, the government (Centre and the states) currently gives to the better-off people plus the 'revenues foregone' in the form of tax concessions and the like given mainly to the corporate sector.

Of course, the better-off people in India—businessmen, rich farmers, the salaried class—will not easily give up on the subsidies they currently enjoy. But this means we should think in terms of mobilising public opinion and activate social movements on a platform like UBI. In particular, as the workers in the informal sector will be the largest beneficiaries of UBI, it can provide a common bridge between them and the unionised formal sector workers, a divide which for many years has weakened the labour movement.

So it will be a pity if Piketty's arguments for a more ambitious egalitarian policy for France, reproduced in *The Wire*, cause a misleading impression against the idea of basic income in India.

THE PANDEMIC AND AFTER

Modi's Theatrics and the Tragedy of India's Poor

Project Syndicate, 21 May 2020

Indian Prime Minister Narendra Modi's penchant for theatrics has had deadly consequences for India's poor. That was certainly the case with his disastrous demonetisation policy in 2016 and his government's rushed implementation of a national Goods and Services Tax (GST), which resulted in widespread harassment for small businesses.

But these flubs were merely the opening act. By imposing one of the world's harshest COVID-19 lockdowns before preparing adequately or consulting with lower levels of government, Modi has inflicted unprecedented damage on India's economy and on the poor, who live hand-to-mouth at the best of times. According to some estimates, more than 120 million people lost their jobs and incomes immediately after the lockdown was ordered on 24 March 2020. And about half of the country's population of 1.38 billion is likely to have been impoverished, with many approaching starvation levels.

Shortly after the lockdown started, India's finance minister, Nirmala Sitharaman, announced a relief package amounting to under 0.5% of GDP. The programme consists primarily of extra food rations, and merely frontloads pre-existing small income grants for farmers, while offering a pittance in cash assistance for women with bank accounts tied to the government's financial inclusion programme, known as Pradhan Mantri Jan Dhan Yojana. And survey data suggest that only about half of India's poor women have Jan Dhan bank accounts.

Then, after seven excruciating weeks, Modi announced with great fanfare on 12 May 2020 that his government would adopt a rescue package worth 10% of GDP. But while this sounds much better than what came before, a closer examination reveals that the amount of immediate relief for the poor remains minimal. That '10% of GDP' includes all the liquidity enhancements announced over the previous three months by the Reserve Bank of India. Worse, most of these funds remain unused, because commercial banks have been unwilling to lend them on to private-sector firms.

The banking sector's stance is understandable. It has been obvious for years that India's economy suffers from deficient demand, which is why it was in a prolonged slowdown before the pandemic arrived. Now that the lockdown is inflicting deep economic losses, an increase in bank lending would most likely do little more than add to the stock of bad loans.

To be sure, the latest rescue package includes a credit guarantee (not actual loans) for 4.5 million microenterprises and small and medium-size businesses (out of a total of 63.4 million across the country). It also includes working-capital assistance for farmers (though many do not have the Kisan Credit Cards required to receive it) and street vendors (though only for about half the ten million in urban India), and a budget increase for rural public works. But, again, while these measures could help to restart disrupted production and supply chains, they will not solve the staggering demand problem (except possibly from the rural works programme).

After weeks of callous disregard for the plight of tens of millions of migrant workers, the government has now announced two months of grain rations. These workers have been hungry and homeless since suddenly losing their jobs, and, with public transportation locked down, many had no choice but to walk hundreds of miles with luggage and children to their villages. Hundreds died on the way.

In general, the government's response has largely excluded hundreds of millions of daily wage labourers and urban workers. A substantial increase in cash assistance to all these people—with or without bank accounts—would have gone a long way towards boosting aggregate demand. Likewise, the government could have done more to discourage major non-farm employers from shedding their workforce, such as by offering a significant wage subsidy for workers on their payrolls (as many other countries, both rich and poor, have done).

The Modi government has also ignored the pressing need for a large-scale transfer of central funds to near-bankrupt state governments that have been covering most of the spending on health care, agriculture, and social protections, and have little capacity to borrow at low cost. Instead, the government's decision-making remains over-centralised, with little participation by local governments and communities, resulting in confusing and conflicting administrative rules.

In a country with a chronically underfunded health system, the immediate priority should have been to invest in a massive public-health programme, particularly at the primary-care level. A government focusing on what really matters would have launched a decentralised programme for testing, contact tracing, and quarantines, while providing special protections for vulnerable populations, such as those over the age of 65 (a mere 6% of the population). This would have allowed for a cautious early relaxation of the lockdown for the rest of the population, who could return to earning a living.

Weighed against the scale of the looming disaster, the government's fiscal response has been pitiably small, still amounting to a mere 1% of GDP or so. Modi and his advisers are probably worried about the government's perceived fiscal rectitude in the eyes of the credit-rating agencies (what some call 'Modi's fear of Moody's'). But not even a high credit rating will stop—let alone reverse—the capital flight currently gripping India; a fiscal chastity belt at a time of economic collapse and widespread destitution is unlikely to help.

Of course, in the medium term, the bill for a larger rescue programme must be paid. This would be painful—but not impossible—with the help of public borrowing, a drastic reduction in subsidies currently benefiting the better off, and a significant increase in taxation. Given that India, a country of extreme wealth inequality, taxes neither wealth nor inheritance, and under-taxes capital gains and real property, plenty of untapped revenue sources are available. A 'corona levy' towards an overhaul of the country's public-health system would also be timely. Needless to say, vested interests will vehemently oppose any new taxes. But there is no better time than a crisis to overcome such resistance.

The great political paradox of contemporary India is that despite all the hardships that Modi has visited upon the poor, he retains considerable popularity among them. A significant portion of the electorate seems to have bought into his fiery rhetoric of muscular Hindu nationalism. (And he certainly hasn't been hurt by the opposition's fecklessness.) Hardly anyone now remembers that in February and March—crucial weeks for pandemic preparation—Modi's party was busy spewing hatred against minorities and dissenters, even as the virus was raging in a neighbouring country.

It is hard to accept that Modi's popularity will remain untarnished by the problems arising from his clumsy mismanagement of the COVID-19 crisis. But if the past is a reliable guide, his hammy bravery against the virus and other elusive enemies may continue to work for him politically, even as it leaves tens of millions of Indians worse off.

Systemic Dysfunctionalities
in Fighting the Virus

Indian Express, 8 April 2020

There have been systemic differences in the way different countries have been fighting the scourge of COVID-19, with different degrees of efficacy. So far reportedly the most successful cases have been in South Korea, Taiwan and Singapore. All these three countries have very effective state machinery, had prepared themselves since the SARS crisis in the early 2000's, and were pro-active in early and mass-testing for infection. Of these South Korea is a centralised democracy, Taiwan a more decentralised civic-participatory democracy, and Singapore is effectively an autocracy. But all these three countries are relatively small, where mass-testing and quarantine are easier to implement.

Take in contrast the virus-fighting performance so far in the largest three countries of the world: China (an openly authoritarian country), India (until recently a democracy, now in an alarming state of decline), and the US (a highly flawed but functioning democracy). China, where the pandemic started, had, after the mismanagement during the SARS epidemic, installed a well-designed early-warning system by which Beijing was to get immediate warning of a contagion developing anywhere in the country. Yet China fumbled again this time, largely because in an authoritarian system the local officials do not want to share bad news with the authorities above. As is well-known by now, Dr Li Wenliang in Wuhan who raised an early alarm in December (and later died of the disease in February) was reprimanded by local officials and made to 'confess' that he was spreading false rumours. This made China (and the world) waste a crucial few weeks. After that initial delay, China quickly mobilised the whole state machinery and put in action a severe quarantine system and, by most accounts, have now largely contained the incidence of the disease (though there are many who do not quite trust the officially released Chinese data). That, of course, has not stopped recent Chinese official propaganda about the superiority of an authoritarian system in fighting the disease. One should not, however, overlook the additional advantage China had in having been the world's leading country in manufacturing and infrastructure construction over the last three decades, which now helped them in speedily building new hospitals and manufacturing ventilators and other medical equipment. This is an advantage which much of the world now lacks, having outsourced it to China for all these years.

In the US, the President and the ruling party have been in denial until mid-March 2020 (consistent with their anti-science and anti-expert attitude), fatally wasting several weeks of preparation, testing and tracing. (A large state where many of the old people live, Florida, under the ruling party did not get going until the beginning of April.) Even in the best of times, the US private medical insurance system is messy, uncoordinated, mired in a bureaucratic system oriented to excluding people, and largely unaffordable for the vast masses of the poor who do not have a stable job. Among rich countries, the system is among the least prepared to face a pandemic of the current proportions. Testing facilities are highly inadequate, nurses are appealing to the general public for donating hand-sewn masks, and already hospitals are facing what is called the triage protocol, when one has to make cruel choices in rationing beds and medical equipment among patients of differing survival probability.

The story behind the dire shortage of ventilators in the US points to a larger systemic issue. More than a decade back the Center for Disease Control asked the Federal government to procure a large number of ventilators in preparation for future emergencies. After considerable search and bidding process, the decision was taken to assign the task of designing and making ventilators to a small California company. Soon after, however, this company was taken over by a corporate giant, which then decided, in view of its multiple product operations, to give low priority to supply the government those ventilators at an agreed low price. It had much bigger fish to fry, and more profitably. So the ventilator project got stalled, and now hospitals have run out of them in the current crisis.

The current regime in India in its health plans has long been trying by and large to copy this American system. Health spending by the Government as percentage of GDP is one of the lowest for a major country, and the public health system is chronically dismal. Faced with the virus, India, like the US, has been woefully unprepared. India also wasted the crucial weeks of February and the first two weeks of March, but not so much because of anti-science attitudes (which are, of course, displayed a-plenty by the ruling party and its affiliates—we all know about cow urine cure and the advice given by a minister for us just to stand in the sun), but more because of another virus that has been afflicting our body politic, the virus of hate and intolerance. Much of February, particular around the time of the Delhi elections, went in hate-mongering against the minority community and all dissenters against the discriminatory citizenship Act; and after the Delhi elections, some ruling party politicians have been busy fomenting riots, for it is widely known that fomenting riots can be a good career move for them in the party.

In the third week of March 2020 came the sudden total lockdown, with hardly any notice or consultation with the state governments, and without any simultaneous announcement about alternative food and shelter arrangements for the suddenly unemployed. The inevitable chaos, police *dandabaji*, displacement and destitution followed. The financial package announced a few days after was a pittance in view of the needs, and about half of the spending announced was old outlays dressed as new, as the millions of the poor are to bang their empty *thali* now in desperation.

One needs more systematic thinking about the hard choices India now faces, the trade-offs between lockdown paralysing the economy and decimating the poor on the one hand, and lifting the lockdown thereby allowing the infection rate to soar, particularly taking a heavy toll on the old, on the other. In a country where the overwhelming majority of the population is young (the median age is somewhere around 26), the trade-off will be different than in western countries where the age composition of the population is drastically different. A wide-ranging public deliberation on these tragic choices is now imperative. I hope our largely sycophantic (electronic) media will now wake up and give scope for this deliberation.

Labour Law Suspension: Hit the Workers when they are Down

Bloomberg Quint, 10 May 2020

Following the piece of age-old wisdom often attributed to Niccolò Machiavelli about not letting a crisis go waste, some state governments in India are busy suspending and diluting labour law protections of workers when the coronavirus crisis and the sudden lockdown that came in its wake are devastating the livelihoods of hundreds of millions of poor workers.

Governments in Uttar Pradesh and Madhya Pradesh are allowing sweeping exemptions from labour laws, including the Industrial Disputes Act and the Factories Act. Echoing the actions of these and a few other state governments, employers' associations are approaching the central government with requests to allow the increase of worker shifts from 8 to 12 hours a day, and the central labour ministry has been receptive.

This, of course, violates an International Labour Organization convention which India had ratified a hundred years back. Except for the Punjab government, other states (for example, Gujarat) have not promised higher overtime wage rates for the extra hours. Besides, very few people pay attention to the fact that longer hours put women workers to great disadvantage, both for their domestic chores and travel safety.

The official justification for such actions has been to encourage investment and employment. For more than a year it has been obvious to most un-blinkered economists that the industrial slowdown is largely due to a slump in demand, and this has now been reinforced by the staggering losses of income during the world's harshest lockdown.

Allowing more intensive exploitation of workers is unlikely to open the sluice gates of investment.

This is comparable to the effects of other recent gifts to business the government has tried. In September 2019, the Finance Minister announced a large reduction in the corporate tax rate, thereby in one stroke slashing government revenues by about Rs 1.5 lakh crore. That happens to be almost double the amount she announced in the form of new programmes for the hundreds of millions of the poor in her first relief package after the lockdown in March. This large gift to the corporate sector did little to relieve the demand problem afflicting investment.

There is significant literature in Indian labour economics on the adverse effects of labour laws. In this, I have, however, never found any convincing demonstration that labour laws particularly those restricting labour retrenchment in firms above a stipulated size even when they have been a constraint, they have actually been a binding constraint. My own explorations into the matter with disaggregated firm-level data have left me sceptical. In recent years, Rajasthan and then 6 or 7 other states have relaxed the stipulated size mentioned above and raised it to firms with more than 300 employees. I have yet to see any rigorous study of this showing a large effect in increasing employment, controlling for other factors. In any case, in recent years in the Indian manufacturing sector, contract labourers (who do not enjoy the job security or social benefits of regular workers) constitute on average at least about one-third of total workers, thereby providing a great deal of labour flexibility, which much of the labour law controversy was about.

GOING THE WRONG WAY

It is interesting that while Indian states are trying to suspend labour protection and make it easier for employers to sack workers, many other countries are trying to minimise lay-offs in this period of crisis by giving wage subsidy to employers to induce them to keep the workers on the payroll. These programmes are an effort to reduce displacement, distress, and loss of worker morale, and at the time of economic recovery less friction and de-skilling. The wage subsidies are quite substantial in Europe, Canada, Australia, and New Zealand. It is also being attempted in some developing countries like Argentina, Bangladesh, Botswana, China, Malaysia, Philippines, South Africa, Thailand, and Turkey. The United States among developed countries and India among developing countries are conspicuous exceptions.

In the continuing sordid saga of callousness and brutality with the millions of suddenly unemployed migrant workers over the last six weeks since lockdown, an interesting fact to note is that employers who mostly had stopped paying them over this period, thus causing widespread hunger and homelessness, have lobbied with state governments to stop sending them back to their villages so that they remain available when the industries restart.

BALANCED REFORM

I am actually in favour of a thorough overhaul. The current labour laws, tangled and outdated as they are, serve the long-term interests of neither the employers nor the workers. At the beginning of this century, the Second National Commission of Labour made a whole set of sensible recommendations for such an overhaul, but they remain largely unimplemented. I would support abolishing the firm size limit on labour retrenchment altogether, provided there is a provision for adequate unemployment benefits, both for regular and contract workers, and there is something like a state-provided Universal Basic Income supplement as a fall-back option for everybody.

Allowing more flexibility in hiring and firing has to be combined, as part of a package deal, with a reasonable scheme of unemployment compensation from an earmarked fund, to which employers and employees should both regularly contribute.

For far too long businesses in India, with some notable exceptions, have considered labour as a necessary but troublesome cog in the production machine, and the focus is to squeeze the maximum out of it with minimum pay and benefits while brandishing the threat of job insecurity. Organised labour, often under politicised partisan leadership from outside, has played that adversarial game. It is in the long-term interests of both sides to see at the ground level that labour-friendly practices can actually enhance long-term productivity and profitability. If cooperation can replace mutual suspicion and labour representatives can be trusted to participate in corporate governance as is the practice, say, in Germany and a few other European countries, labour organisations can play a responsible role in achieving mutually beneficial goals. Taking the cover of the pandemic to unilaterally whittle down labour protections is going the opposite way, to distrust, and labour unrest.

A Proposed Economic Relief Package

Economic Times, 22 April 2020

The lockdown of 24 March 2020—that came after inordinate delay (7 weeks after the WHO declaration of a global public health emergency) and with gratuitous suddenness, with no preparation or consultation with the state governments or consideration of the immediate hardships for the poor (not to speak of the police *dandabaji* in its enforcement)—is clearly having a severe economic impact. The job and income losses have been staggering. There are no good estimates but hundreds of millions may have been affected, the overwhelming majority of whom live a daily hand-to-mouth existence even at the best of times, and cannot afford remote working from home, social distancing or the luxuries of frequent hand-washing with soap.

In this article, I shall briefly talk about (A) the immediate broad measures of relief needed for the poor; (B) taking the opportunity of the corona crisis to turn some of the relief measures into more fundamental changes in our patchy welfare system; and (C) some indications about how to get resources to pay the large bill.

(A)

1. At a time when the specter of hunger is stalking the land, one has to mobilise a network of community kitchens throughout the country (at the moment they are more in South than in North India), administered by local civic bodies and voluntary organisations or NGOs. For this purpose, the current harsh and harassing restrictions of FCRA should be relaxed (in any case these restrictions are arbitrary when all political parties are exempt from this Act, even retrospectively).

2. Cash assistance to a much larger extent than announced by the Government so far, and to both men and women.

3. Universal public distribution of foodgrains to whoever needs food (relieving the over-full FCI warehouses, even before the rabi crop arrives). Not having a ration or Aadhaar card should not be a barrier. Now is not the time to worry about undue 'leakage' or 'inclusion error'.

4. Open up all marketing channels for farm produce (including direct farmer-to-buyer sales), going beyond the existing cartelised mandi system.

5. Along with restarting NREGA in a COVID-safe way in the rural areas (where the problems of delayed wage payment and unmet demand for work in some areas need to be resolved), it is urgent to start on similar lines an *urban employment guarantee scheme* on public works and civic programmes, as our urban infrastructure has been in shambles. This can employ hundreds of thousands of migrant workers who are still stranded, other workers in services and retail trade suddenly jobless, plus the very large numbers (the world's largest) of under-trial prisoners, who have rotted in jail for years (because they could not afford bail), now to be released to mitigate the virus danger in our prisons—at least the able-bodied ones among them.

6. Debt moratorium for and intensive infusion of credit to all financially fragile micro and small businesses.

7. Actively discourage all major employers to lay off their workers (including their contract workers), and offer in return a significant *wage subsidy* for all workers on their payroll (as some North European countries are doing), using Aadhaar card identification to avoid fake payrolls.

(B)

The current pandemic points attention to the woeful inadequacies of the Government's flagship Ayushman Bharat programme or any other subsidised primarily private insurance system on the American model. One needs a universal health care system with a much larger role of the public health system and at least a trebling of the current pitifully low Government health-spending-to-GDP ratio. (Even the virus-testing in private clinics now is unaffordable for large numbers of people, who may not be all extremely poor, with its obvious effects on infection-spreading.) We should take the opportunity given by the crisis to carry out a complete overhaul of our public health system in the medium term.

Similarly, the cash assistance programme should be broadened and systematised into an unconditional Universal Basic Income supplement that can provide economic security as a citizen's fundamental right. The PM-KISAN programme has been a small step in that direction, but it excludes vast numbers of landless labourers and non-farmers and the amount dispensed is too small.

(C)

All this is surely going to cost a lot of money. Right now, over the next 6 months or so, fiscal rectitude cannot be our priority. Along with public borrowing from domestic and foreign sources, monetise much of the deficit, if necessary. Inflation is not on the immediate scenario. Forget about credit-rating agencies—even their high ratings will not stem the tide of capital outflow; and a fiscal chastity-belt at a time of economic collapse and widespread destitution is unlikely to improve our ratings.

In the medium run, we have to worry about our extreme public resource scarcity. There exist viable schemes of significant taxation of wealth, inheritance, capital gains and property values in a country of extreme wealth inequality, that can *potentially* raise nearly 2% of GDP. It has also been estimated that elimination of central and state subsidies (like those on power and fertilisers) that benefit mainly the better-off, and of a fraction of current tax concessions to companies ('revenues foregone' in budget parlance) can *potentially* raise another 7% of GDP. These measures will, of course, be resisted by politically powerful vested interests, but a crisis is the most opportune time to fight such resistance.

Decentralise Relief Policy

Business Standard, 29 April 2020

In fighting the onslaught of the coronavirus in this large country, policy measures have to be different in different areas, depending on the patterns of infection spread and livelihoods disrupted. Yet, much of the policy so far has been over-centralised, with the initial lockdown decision taken by the central leadership without consulting state-level leaders and with an unnecessary suddenness that left little time for preparation and caused enormous hardships for millions of poor workers. It has also been enforced not through building community-level trust, but with characteristically harsh police crackdowns, callousness for the stranded migrant workers, and rigidity of top-down rules (the Kerala state government which has done an exemplary job of containing the disease was chastised for attempted non-conformity with by-then out-dated central lockdown rules). Some flexibility has now been promised for state governments after 3 May 2020. But this is not enough for the regional policy diversity needed.

If one looks at the country-wide dispersion of the *infection 'hotspots'*, there is a broad pattern. They are mostly in urban centres and in economically better-off regions of India (maybe because of their larger global connections and surely because of urban density). Clearly in these areas stringent lockdown plus testing and tracing have to be continued for some time. This is also because density and slum conditions make social distancing harder to implement.

But in large parts of north-central and eastern India infection has been much less so far. These are areas where India's poor are concentrated to a large extent. These are also by and large areas where demographic trends and fertility rates have made the population much younger (the fraction of the virus-vulnerable older age-groups is smaller). This means, the *economic 'hot-spots'*—where the precariousness of the hand-to-mouth existence of the poor is likely to be more severe, with large proportions of the youth unemployed or under-employed—may be larger in numbers in these areas. So here the emphasis has to be primarily on economic relief for the poor and recovery policies for agriculture and informal-sector small and micro enterprises.

The cash crunch in buying of various agricultural inputs (before the coming kharif season) and the credit crunch for the enterprises need to be relieved. For the marketing of the in-coming *rabi* crop, one needs to open up all marketing channels for farm produce (including direct farmer-to-buyer sales), going beyond the existing cartelised *mandi* system. Inter-state, as well as intra-state, public and private transport of goods should be opened up, without too much problems in maintaining some social-distancing rules in roads and markets.

Cash assistance to a much larger extent than announced by the Government so far, and to both men and women, with or without bank accounts, has to be arranged. NREGA programmes need to be fully reactivated, and the frequent problems of delayed wage payment and unmet demand for work need to be resolved. For the millions of people who are still outside the public food distribution system, grains released from the over-full FCI warehouses should be distributed, without any requirement for ration or Aadhaar card.

Unless the infection geography changes significantly, the state governments in these north-central and eastern regions may thus be a bit more relaxed on the lockdown and focus on economic issues. Also, in predominantly rural areas social distancing is less difficult to implement, particularly if panchayats and community organisations are mobilised in spreading messages about appropriate public hygiene practices. Schools should be kept open—cautiously; one has to keep in mind that the school meal is often the only major meal for the children. In any case, as we have mentioned, the age-group composition is usually such that the disease-vulnerability (except through malnutrition) may be somewhat less (although, one has to keep in mind that the public health system to take care of the diseased is much weaker in these areas). One has to combine less stringent lockdown with a more active policy of local primary health workers paying special attention to the old and the infirm in regular household visits.

In the more infected, more urban, disease 'hotspots', the immediate economic relief policies to be taken are quite clear. The particular focus should be on the stranded migrant workers, the suddenly-unemployed street vendors and other self-employed and wage workers (and, if our prisons are to be de-congested in the time of the virus, the released masses of under-trial prisoners). For these people, apart from mobilising a network of community kitchens and also making sure that the promised cash assistance (even if workers do not have a bank account) and enhanced rations of food (even if the migrant workers do not have their ration cards) reach them, immediate debt-forgiveness and infusion of new credit need to be arranged for those with small business. In addition, a new programme of *urban employment guarantee* on public works and other civic projects should be immediately started to provide alternative employment to at least those who do not want to go back to their villages. Moreover, a pro-active policy is called for to discourage all major factory employers from laying off their workers (including their contract workers), and offer in return a significant *wage subsidy* for all workers on their payroll (as some North European countries are doing), using, if necessary, Aadhaar card identification to avoid fake payrolls.

The central Government so far has been quite stingy in announcing an economic relief package. Only about half of the announced first package contained new programmes (amounting to less than 0.5% of GDP). The total package needed, by many accounts, should cost 10 times that much. At a time of looming economic and humanitarian catastrophe, fiscal rectitude cannot be our priority.

Also, since much of the spending on health, agriculture, and social protection has to be incurred by the states, much needs to be done in clearing the GST arrears, in making the rules of financial allocation in central programmes more flexible, and immediately creating an infrastructure for financial transfer and coordination between the central and state governments (in this respect I endorse the recommendation made by the Centre for Policy Research of a new emergency set-up under the hitherto-dormant Inter-State Council).

The Politics of Fiscal Apathy

Scroll.in, 12 June 2020

Several economists and businessmen have expressed their disappointment with the contents of the financial package announced by the government to face the unprecedented economic crisis brought about by the COVID-19-induced lockdown, the suddenness and severity of which had itself surprised many epidemiologists.

The callousness towards the migrants and lack of immediate preparation to send them back—or at least feed and house them—before the lockdown have shocked many. The financial package includes many liquidity enhancement policies already announced by the Reserve Bank of India and new loan guarantees that are unlikely to be effective when demand deficiency discourages producers to take loans.

It also includes some otherwise-desirable structural reform proposals, like those for agricultural marketing, power distribution companies or privatisation of inefficient public enterprises. But as is well known, a fire outbreak is not the best time to sit down and talk about reforming the ways of running the fire station.

While the hype was about 10% of Gross Domestic Product, the fiscal package contained immediate relief of not much more than 1% of the GDP.

THE CASE FOR CASH INFUSION

In view of the severe job and income losses faced by the poor, many economists have stressed the need for larger cash assistance to those who do not have bank accounts. This can be done by sending a money-order by post or even dispensing cash with indelible ink on finger—particularly to urban workers and street vendors.

There should also be provisions for owners of micro, small and medium enterprises—one-third of which, surveys indicate, are beyond recovery—and wage subsidies to employers to discourage lay-offs. Instead, our rule-bound bureaucrats have been obsessed with inclusion error—that of money going to some non-poor people, even as hunger stalks the land.

While state governments are on the frontline of the public health battle, and social protection and agriculture and are near-bankrupt, the Central government has been very stingy in arranging for large and necessary fiscal transfers, starting with Goods and Services Tax arrears and shortfalls. The states will also be hurt by cuts in centrally-sponsored schemes. Even the corporate social responsibility donations can go to PM-CARES fund, but not to the Chief Ministers' Relief Funds—chief ministers supposedly don't care enough.

POLITICS BEHIND THE APATHY

The raging question is why has the Central government in India been so tight-fisted, compared to many other countries? It is worth examining some of the usual political-economy rationales offered.

Even though the majority of academic and policy economists have asked for a more generous rescue package, there are fiscal conservatives in and around the government who are worried about the inflationary consequences of large fiscal deficits, particularly with tax revenues declining. The United Progressive Alliance government had a much larger rescue package after the 2008-09 financial crisis, but what lingers is the memory of its inability to control the inflation in later years and the electoral price it paid.

During the financial crisis, some countries in Europe and elsewhere that adopted serious austerity policies, suffered severe adverse consequences, particularly for their poor workers. In India, under the current conditions of large food stocks and foreign exchange reserves and low international oil prices, inflation is not on the immediate horizon. The more the economic recovery is delayed by austere fiscal policies, the more acute will be the revenue shortfall and debt problem.

Of course, we are now facing both supply and demand constraints, but the supply constraints are likely to ease up much earlier—as the agricultural sector and rural areas have been significantly less affected by coronavirus than metropolitan areas, and as transport bottlenecks clear with the unlocking of the economy. Meanwhile, the demand deficiency problem will loom large. The supply constraint would also have been alleviated by more cash infusion, not just loan guarantees, into the micro, small and medium enterprises sector.

Large-scale public borrowing, both domestic and foreign is called for. As many as 66 countries have already received emergency financial assistance from the International Monetary Fund, while India has not even asked for it. The necessary fiscal space can be created to pay it back in the medium term by fresh taxation—such as wealth, inheritance and carbon taxes, for instance—and reduction of large subsidies that now primarily go to the better-off. Those who insist that there is no fiscal space are directly or indirectly covering for vested interests, expecting the poor to quietly bear the brunt.

Another possible reason for the relative fiscal apathy of the Central government for the poor may be that after the lifting of the lockdown, the problem is now in the hands of state governments. If things do not work out, they can be blamed. Moreover, the tragedy of the migrant workers may be politically tolerable, as they don't usually vote at their places of migration. But some of the state governments run by the Bharatiya Janata Party—in power at the Centre—are also suffering from the resource crunch, and many migrants are going back to states run by the ruling party or its allies.

There may also be some overconfidence in the ruling party. After all, they have successfully overcome, with electoral impunity, earlier policy blunders—like demonetisation and implementation of the Goods and Services Tax—that also ended up assaulting mainly the poor. Then there is always the ultimate resort: the supreme leader's magical oratory and some national security-related patriotic circus to go with it.

The Two Largest Democracies
in the World are the Sickest Now

Scroll.in, 24 August 2020

The two largest democracies in the world, India and the United States, are now struggling and flailing in the fight against the Coronavirus. India has the world's largest number of new cases, followed closely by the US. The number of reported cases are almost surely undercounts, as in both countries testing has been delayed and highly inadequate, if not downright chaotic. Death rates per million people are much lower in India, possibly because the Indian population is much younger. As the number of cases mounted, the government in both countries discontinued giving daily briefings on the virus impact.

As is well known, in the US, President Donald Trump and his party had been in denial or claiming imminent victories too often (consistent with their anti-science and anti-expert attitude), fatally wasting several weeks of potential preparation. Simple hygienic precautionary measures have been politicised, with not wearing masks becoming a sign of partisan or libertarian defiance.

The US also lacks a unified public health agency to authoritatively handle and coordinate in a major pandemic. Even in the best of times, the US private medical insurance system is messy, uncoordinated, mired in a bureaucratic system oriented to exclude people, and largely unaffordable for all those, particularly the poor, who do not have a stable job. Among rich countries, the system is among the least prepared to face a pandemic of the current proportions.

The current regime in India, in its health plans, has been trying by and large to copy the American system of subsidised private insurance. Health spending by the Indian government as percentage of GDP has long been one of the lowest for any major country, and the public health system is chronically dismal. This has been a matter of national shame, but this kind of shame does not get the attention of our current crop of ultra-nationalists.

A POORLY HANDLED PANDEMIC

Faced with the virus, India, like the US, has been woefully unprepared. India also wasted crucial weeks in February and March 2020, even as the virus was raging in a neighbouring country. This was not so much because of anti-science attitudes (though they are not absent in the ruling party and its affiliates— remember the cow urine drinking parties organised by some of them to forestall the virus), but more because of another virus that has been afflicting India's body politic: the virus of hate and intolerance.

Much of February, particularly around the time of the Delhi state elections, went in majoritarian hate-mongering against the minority Muslim community and all dissenters against the highly discriminatory Citizenship (Amendment) Act, 2019 (CAA). The protesting women of Shaheen Bagh were the enemy, more than the pandemic. On 24 February 2020, the regime felicitated Trump in an Ahmedabad cricket stadium packed with 110,000 people, at a time when restrictions were already in place in some countries. After the Delhi elections, some ruling party politicians were busy fomenting riots. In the first half of March, the central leadership was preoccupied with toppling an Opposition state government.

In the third week of March came the sudden total lockdown, among the world's most stringent, when Prime Minister Narendra Modi asked the nation for only three weeks' time for victory in the war against the virus. The lockdown came with hardly any notice or consultation with the state governments, and without any simultaneous announcement about alternative food and shelter arrangements for the suddenly unemployed. The inevitable chaos, police excesses in enforcement, displacement and destitution followed.

Since then, the central bureaucracy, in its typical heavy-handed way, issued thousands of arbitrary and often-conflicting regulations. There have been also cases of ruling-party politicians and health officials scapegoating minority Muslim communities as super-spreaders (as with immigrants in Trump's America, or Jews in medieval plague-ridden European cities).

By now the whole matter of fighting both the health and the economic crises has been relegated to the state governments, which are at the frontline of the battle without adequate financial help or technical assistance, as in the US. Meanwhile, infection rates are galloping and are expected by some epidemiologists to reach over a hundred million by the end of the year.

The Indian government has tried to distract public attention from the massive-scale human suffering brought about by the pandemic and the economic paralysis, with religious spectacles harking back to ancient myths of pious glory, with the Prime Minister acting as the high priest, on a site of fanatic vandalism now court-sanctioned.

The government in the US has tried to distract attention by sending federal troops to intimidate largely peaceful protesters. In both countries, chaos has reigned with the lack of federal coordination in mobilising finance and technical expertise, in allocating scarce medical resources across regions, and in aligning travel restrictions with lockdowns and openings, as the virus surges in different regions at different times.

A CRISIS OF DEMOCRACY

All this is grist to the mill of Chinese propaganda that their authoritarian state is better at handling the pandemic than the 'western' democratic system. China, of course, initially fumbled (as they also did during the SARS crisis in 2003) in Wuhan, and thereby wasted crucial weeks both for itself and the world, largely because in an authoritarian system the local officials are reluctant to share bad news with the authorities above. Since then they have mobilised the state machinery reasonably well in curbing the disease, though the official data on death rates are dubious.

The Chinese propaganda also deliberately ignores the successful examples in democratic countries like Germany, Austria, Denmark, New Zealand, Uruguay, Costa Rica, and in their immediate neighbourhood, Taiwan and South Korea. Incidentally, the idea of democracy is not exclusively 'western'. There are some 'eastern' examples even in the ancient world, like in the Buddhist discourse and practice of public deliberation and decision-making in ancient Indian city republics, almost around the same time when western democracy is traced to Greece, and also in ancient Mesopotamia.

An effective and well-coordinated state is important in handling crisis, but authoritarianism is neither necessary nor sufficient for this. The dysfunctionalities in the two largest democracies are not inherent to the process of democracy as such. In fact, some of the problems those two countries are facing are partly because they had enfeebled some institutions of democratic responsibility and accountability. (The Swedish V-Dem Institute's well-known *Democracy Report* shows a large decline in democracy index both for India and the US in recent years). Both governments have used the cover of the virus to try to criminalise protests and dilute environmental regulations.

One major difference in the two democracies is that political opposition to the government's mishandling of the crisis is much more energised and organised in the US now, with some hope for democratic rejuvenation in the near future. Unfortunately, such hope is absent in India.

There is a danger that by the time the Coronavirus crisis is finally over in India, there may be only a largely hollowed-out shell of democracy left. India will then be known as the world's largest pseudo-democracy. This will give China a much larger ideological victory than their minor military one at India's borders that the Indian government is currently busy covering up to prop its faltering image of muscular nationalism.

Index

www.ingramcontent.com/pod-product-compliance
Lightning Source LLC
Chambersburg PA
CBHW042116190326
41519CB00030B/7521